OFFICIAL SQA PAST PAPERS WITH SQA ANSWERS

Higher
PHYSICS

**Higher Grade 1998 to 1999,
and Higher Still Specimen Question Paper,
2000 and 2001 with three years' answers**

First exam published in 1998.

Published by
Leckie & Leckie Ltd, 8 Whitehill Terrace, St. Andrews, Scotland KY16 8RN
tel: 01334 475656 fax: 01334 477392
hq@leckieandleckie.co.uk www.leckieandleckie.co.uk

Leckie & Leckie Project Management Team: Tom Davie; David Nicoll; Bruce Ryan
Cover Design Assistance: Mike Middleton

ISBN 1-84372-013-2

A CIP Catalogue record for this book is available from the British Library.

Printed in Scotland by Inglis Allen on environmentally friendly paper. The paper is made
from a mixture of sawmill waste, forest thinnings and wood from sustainable forests.

® Leckie & Leckie is a registered trademark.

Leckie & Leckie Ltd achieved the Investors in People Standard in 1999.

Leckie & Leckie

Introduction

The best way to prepare for exams is to practise, again and again, all that you have learned over the past year. Work through these questions and check your solutions against these *official SQA answers*. But give yourself a real chance and be honest! Make sure you work through each question thoroughly so that you understand how you got the right answer – *you will have to do this in the exam!*

Although the 1998 and 1999 Papers cover the old Higher Grade exam, you will still find them useful for your Higher Still revision.

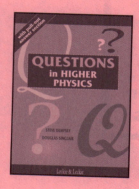

Higher Physics Revision Notes. An experienced teacher shares his expertise, breaking the course down into four pointer areas. This logical approach is coupled with sound advice on how to study. Make this a fulcrum for your knowledge.

Questions in Higher Physics. 206 questions are the downforce you must overcome. But sizeable upthrust is available by regularly reviewing these exercises. Gain the momentum you need as you complete the study circuit.

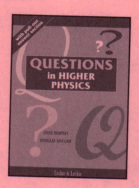

Contents

3220/201

SCOTTISH
CERTIFICATE OF
EDUCATION
1998

FRIDAY, 15 MAY
9.30 AM – 11.00 AM

PHYSICS
HIGHER GRADE
Paper I

Read Carefully

1 All questions should be attempted.

2 The following data should be used when required unless otherwise stated.

Speed of light in vacuum c	$3 \cdot 00 \times 10^{8}$ m s^{-1}	Planck's constant h	$6 \cdot 63 \times 10^{-34}$ J s
Charge on electron e	$-1 \cdot 60 \times 10^{-19}$ C	Mass of electron m_e	$9 \cdot 11 \times 10^{-31}$ kg
Acceleration due to gravity g	$9 \cdot 8$ m s^{-2}	Mass of proton m_p	$1 \cdot 67 \times 10^{-27}$ kg

Section A (questions 1 to 30)

3 Check that the answer sheet is for Physics Higher I (Section A).

4 Answer the questions numbered 1 to 30 on the answer sheet provided.

5 Fill in the details required on the answer sheet.

6 Rough working, if required, should be done only on this question paper, or on the first two pages of the answer book provided—**not** on the answer sheet.

7 For each of the questions 1 to 30 there is only **one** correct answer and each is worth 1 mark.

8 Instructions as to how to record your answers to questions 1–30 are given on page two.

Section B (questions 31 to 37)

9 Answer questions numbered 31 to 37 in the answer book provided.

10 Fill in the details on the front of the answer book.

11 Enter the question number clearly in the margin of the answer book beside each of your answers to questions 31 to 37.

12 Care should be taken **not** to give an unreasonable number of significant figures in the final answers to calculations.

SCOTTISH
QUALIFICATIONS
AUTHORITY

SECTION A

For questions 1 to 30 in this section of the paper, an answer is recorded on the answer sheet by indicating the choice A, B, C, D or E by a stroke made in ink in the appropriate box of the answer sheet—see the example below.

EXAMPLE

The energy unit measured by the electricity meter in your home is the

    A ampere

    B kilowatt-hour

    C watt

    D coulomb

    E volt.

The correct answer to the question is B—kilowatt-hour. Record your answer by drawing a heavy vertical line joining the two dots in the appropriate box on your answer sheet in the column of boxes headed B. The entry on your answer sheet would now look like this:

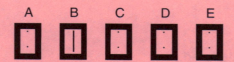

If after you have recorded your answer you decide that you have made an error and wish to make a change, you should cancel the original answer and put a vertical stroke in the box you now consider to be correct. Thus, if you want to change an answer D to an answer B, your answer sheet would look like this:

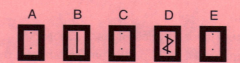

If you want to change back to an answer which has already been scored out, you should enter a tick (✓) to the RIGHT of the box of your choice, thus:

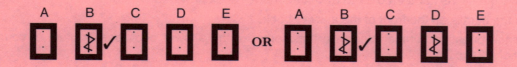

SECTION A

Answer questions 1–30 on the answer sheet.

1. Consider the following three statements made by pupils about scalars and vectors.

   I Scalars have direction only.

   II Vectors have both size and direction.

   III Speed is a scalar and velocity is a vector.

   Which statement(s) is/are true?

   A I only

   B I and II only

   C I and III only

   D II and III only

   E I, II and III

2. The following is a speed-time graph of the beginning of a cyclist's journey along a straight track.

   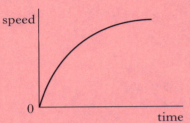

   Which of the following could be the corresponding acceleration-time graph for the same period?

   A

   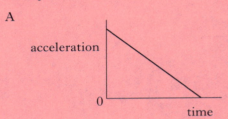

   B

   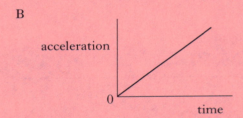

   C

   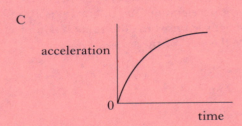

   D

   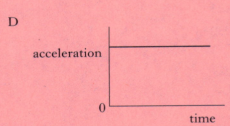

   E

   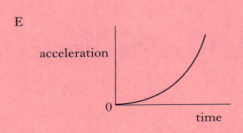

3. A cyclist is travelling along a straight, level road at $10 \, m\,s^{-1}$. She applies her brakes and comes to rest after travelling a further 20 m.

   The braking force is constant. What is her deceleration?

   A $0\cdot25 \, m\,s^{-2}$

   B $0\cdot50 \, m\,s^{-2}$

   C $2\cdot0 \, m\,s^{-2}$

   D $2\cdot5 \, m\,s^{-2}$

   E $5\cdot0 \, m\,s^{-2}$

4. A stone is thrown horizontally with a speed of $12 \, m\,s^{-1}$ over the edge of a vertical cliff. It hits the sea at a horizontal distance of 60 m out from the base of the cliff.

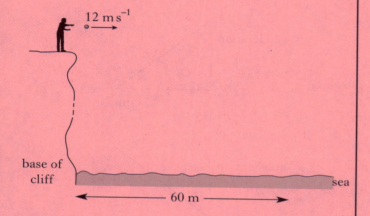

   Assuming that air resistance is negligible and that the acceleration due to gravity is $10 \, m\,s^{-2}$, the height from which the stone was projected above the level of the sea is

   A   5 m

   B   25 m

   C   50 m

   D   125 m

   E   250 m.

5. A rocket of mass 200 kg accelerates vertically upwards from the surface of a planet at $2 \, m\,s^{-2}$.

   The gravitational field strength on the planet is $4 \, N\,kg^{-1}$.

   What is the size of the force being supplied by the rocket's engines?

   A   800 N

   B   1200 N

   C   2000 N

   D   2400 N

   E   4800 N

6. Two boys are pulling a car of mass 800 kg along a level surface with a pair of ropes attached horizontally as shown below.

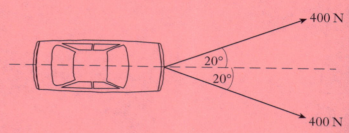

   When the pull on each rope is 400 N in the directions indicated, the acceleration of the car is $0\cdot1 \, m\,s^{-2}$.

   What is the size of the frictional force acting on the car in the above situation?

   A   194 N

   B   434 N

   C   533 N

   D   672 N

   E   832 N

7. A block of mass 1 kg slides along a frictionless surface at 10 m s⁻¹ and it collides with a stationary block of mass 10 kg. After the collision, the first block rebounds at 5 m s⁻¹ and the other one moves off at 1·5 m s⁻¹.

before impact

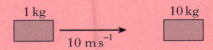

after impact

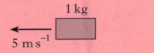

Which row in the following table is correct?

	Momentum of system	Kinetic energy of system	Type of collision
A	conserved	conserved	elastic
B	conserved	not conserved	inelastic
C	conserved	not conserved	elastic
D	not conserved	not conserved	inelastic
E	not conserved	not conserved	elastic

8. Which pair of graphs correctly shows how the pressure produced by a liquid depends on the depth and the density of the liquid?

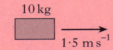

[Turn over

9. The pressure-volume graph below describes the behaviour of a constant mass of gas when it is heated.

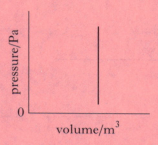

Which of the following shows the corresponding pressure-temperature graph?

A

B

C

D

E

10. A balloon of mass 10 kg accelerates vertically upwards with a constant acceleration of $1\,\mathrm{m\,s}^{-2}$. The air resistance acting on the balloon is 100 N.

Assuming that the acceleration due to gravity is $10\,\mathrm{m\,s}^{-2}$, which row in the following table shows the size and direction of the forces acting on the balloon?

	Weight	Air resistance	Upthrust
A	↓ 100 N	↓ 100 N	↑ 200 N
B	↓ 100 N	↓ 100 N	↑ 210 N
C	↓ 100 N	↑ 100 N	↑ 10 N
D	↓ 10 N	↓ 100 N	↑ 120 N
E	↓ 100 N	↑ 100 N	↑ 100 N

11. In the circuit below, each resistor has a resistance of $20\,\Omega$ and the battery has negligible internal resistance.

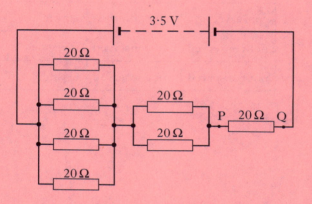

The voltage across PQ is

A   0·5 V

B   1·0 V

C   1·5 V

D   2·0 V

E   3·5 V.

12. A battery, of e.m.f. 15 V and internal resistance 5 Ω, is connected to two 10 Ω resistors as shown. Switch S is initially open.

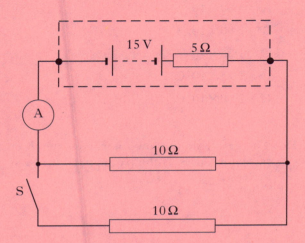

When switch S is closed, the reading on the ammeter changes

A   from 1 A to 2 A

B   from 1·5 A to 3 A

C   from 1 A to 1·5 A

D   from 1·5 A to 0·75 A

E   from 1 A to 0·6 A.

13. A student sets up the following potential divider circuit which includes a light-dependent resistor (LDR).

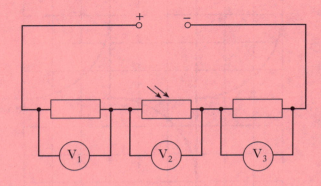

The resistance of the LDR decreases when the light intensity on it increases.

Which row in the table below correctly shows how the voltmeter readings are affected when the student switches off all the lights in the laboratory?

	Reading on voltmeter V_1	Reading on voltmeter V_2	Reading on voltmeter V_3
A	increases	increases	increases
B	decreases	decreases	decreases
C	increases	decreases	increases
D	decreases	increases	decreases
E	no change	increases	no change

14. In the Wheatstone bridge shown below, there is a small reading on the voltmeter.

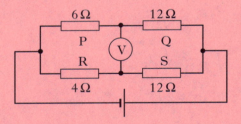

What should be done to balance the Wheatstone bridge?

A   Increase the value of resistor P by 6 Ω.

B   Increase the value of resistor Q by 6 Ω.

C   Increase the value of resistor R by 6 Ω.

D   Increase the value of resistor S by 6 Ω.

E   Insert a 6 Ω resistor in series with the voltmeter.

15. The output from an electrical device produces the following trace on an oscilloscope.

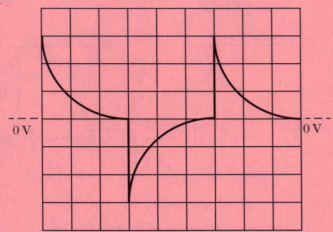

The time-base setting of the oscilloscope is 2 ms per division and the voltage-gain setting is 5 mV per division.

What is the frequency and maximum voltage of the output from this electrical device?

	Frequency of the device/Hz	Maximum voltage output from the device/mV
A	33	15
B	83	15
C	83	30
D	166	30
E	166	15

16. What is the relationship between the r.m.s. and peak values for an alternating current?

A $I_{r.m.s.} = \dfrac{I_p}{\sqrt{2}}$

B $I_{r.m.s.} = \sqrt{2}\, I_p$

C $I_{r.m.s.} = 2\, I_p^2$

D $I_{r.m.s.} = \dfrac{\sqrt{I_p}}{2}$

E $I_{r.m.s.} = \dfrac{I_p^2}{2}$

17. A 25 μF capacitor is charged until the potential difference across it is 500 V. The charge stored in the capacitor is

A $5.00 \times 10^{-8}\,C$

B $2.00 \times 10^{-5}\,C$

C $1.25 \times 10^{-2}\,C$

D $1.25 \times 10^{4}\,C$

E $2.00 \times 10^{7}\,C.$

18. The graph shows how the charge stored on a capacitor varies as the p.d. applied across it is increased.

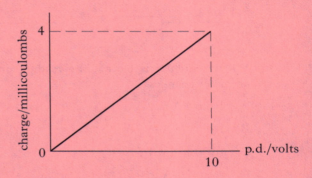

What is the energy stored in the capacitor when the p.d. across it is 10 V?

A   0·4 mJ

B   2·5 mJ

C   10 mJ

D   20 mJ

E   40 mJ

19. In the circuits shown below, P and Q are identical lamps and the a.c. supplies have the same r.m.s. voltage output. The lamps glow with equal brightness.

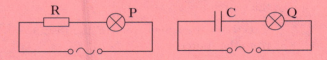

The frequency of each supply voltage is increased without altering the value of the r.m.s. voltage output.

Which row in the following table correctly describes how the brightness of each lamp is affected?

	Lamp P	Lamp Q
A	brighter	unchanged
B	unchanged	brighter
C	dimmer	unchanged
D	unchanged	dimmer
E	dimmer	brighter

20. The amplifier shown below is operating in the differential mode.

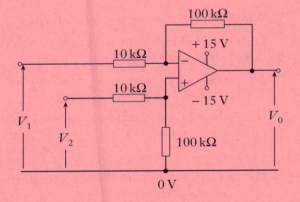

When $V_0 = 0.60\,V$ and $V_1 = 2.70\,V$, what is the value of V_2?

A   2·10 V

B   2·16 V

C   2·76 V

D   3·30 V

E   3·36 V

21. The diagram below shows a ray of light from a laser passing from air into glass and then into water.

The refractive index of glass is greater than that of water.

Which is the correct path for the light?

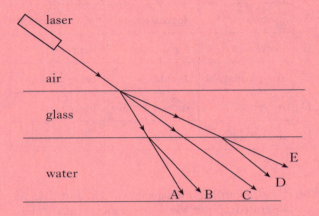

22. A ray of light travelling through glass approaches air, as shown below.

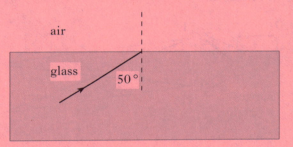

The refractive index of the glass is 1·5.

Which of the following paths will the ray follow?

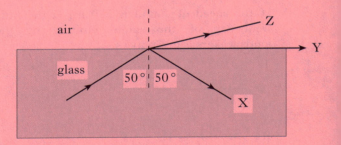

A   X only

B   Y only

C   Z only

D   X and Z only

E   Y and Z only

[Turn over

23. Light travels from air into glass.

Which row in the following table correctly describes what happens to the speed, frequency and wavelength of the light?

	Speed	Frequency	Wavelength
A	increases	decreases	stays constant
B	decreases	stays constant	decreases
C	stays constant	decreases	decreases
D	increases	stays constant	increases
E	decreases	decreases	stays constant

24. Two identical loudspeakers, L_1 and L_2, are operated at the same frequency and in phase with each other by connecting them in parallel across the output of a signal generator, as shown below. A sound interference pattern is produced.

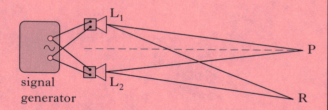

At position P, which is the same distance from both loudspeakers, a microphone registers a maximum intensity of sound.

The next maximum is registered at position R, where $L_1R = 4 \cdot 6$ m and $L_2R = 4 \cdot 3$ m.

If the speed of sound is 330 m s^{-1}, then the frequency of the sound emitted by the loudspeakers is given by

A $\dfrac{(4 \cdot 6 - 4 \cdot 3)}{330}$ Hz

B $\dfrac{330}{(4 \cdot 6 + 4 \cdot 3)}$ Hz

C $\dfrac{330}{(4 \cdot 6 - 4 \cdot 3)}$ Hz

D $330 \times (4 \cdot 6 - 4 \cdot 3)$ Hz

E $330 \times (4 \cdot 6 + 4 \cdot 3)$ Hz.

25. The intensity of radiation emitted from a point source of light varies

A   directly as the distance from the source

B   directly as the square of the distance from the source

C   directly as the square root of the distance from the source

D   inversely as the distance from the source

E   inversely as the square of the distance from the source.

26. Certain materials can be "doped" to make a semiconductor called an n-type material.

In an n-type material,

A   the majority charge carriers are electrons

B   the majority charge carriers are neutrons

C   the majority charge carriers are protons

D   there are more electrons than protons

E   there are more electrons than neutrons.

27. The symbols for two isotopes of carbon, carbon 14 and carbon 12, are as follows.

Which of the following statements is true?

Carbon 14 and carbon 12 are said to be isotopes of carbon because

A   carbon 14 has the same mass number as carbon 12

B   carbon 14 has a different atomic number from carbon 12

C   carbon 14 is radioactive

D   carbon 14 has the same number of neutrons as carbon 12

E   carbon 14 and carbon 12 have different mass numbers but the same atomic number.

28. Two different types of tinted glass, X and Y, are used to make filters for sunglasses. A sample of each glass is placed in turn between a source and a detector, as shown in the following diagram. Both samples are identical in size and shape.

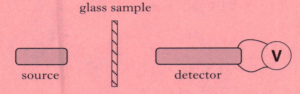

glass sample

source   detector

The source emits electromagnetic radiation with a wide range of wavelengths, all of the same intensity as shown below.

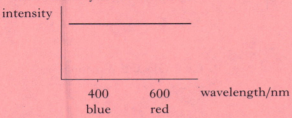

intensity

400   600   wavelength/nm
blue   red

The following graphs show the intensities measured by the detector after the electromagnetic radiation passed through each of the glass samples.

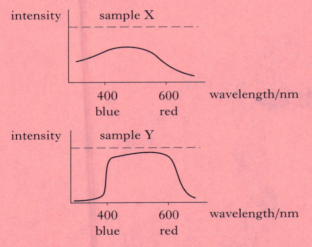

intensity   sample X

400   600   wavelength/nm
blue   red

intensity   sample Y

400   600   wavelength/nm
blue   red

Which of the following statement(s) is/are correct?

I   Sample X is better at absorbing red light than sample Y.

II   Sample Y is better at protecting the eye from ultraviolet radiation.

III The view would appear darker when seen through sample Y than when seen through sample X.

A   I only

B   I and II only

C   I and III only

D   II and III only

E   I, II and III

29. There are a number of equations involving the following quantities.

A, the activity of a radioactive source

D, the absorbed dose

H, the dose equivalent

$\dot{H}$, the dose equivalent rate

Q, the quality factor

N, the number of nuclei decaying

t, the time

Which row of the following table states **three** of these equations correctly?

A	$A = \dfrac{N}{t}$	$H = DQ$	$\dot{H} = Ht$
B	$A = Nt$	$H = DQ$	$\dot{H} = \dfrac{H}{t}$
C	$A = \dfrac{N}{t}$	$H = \dfrac{D}{Q}$	$\dot{H} = Ht$
D	$A = Nt$	$H = \dfrac{D}{Q}$	$\dot{H} = \dfrac{H}{t}$
E	$A = \dfrac{N}{t}$	$H = DQ$	$\dot{H} = \dfrac{H}{t}$

30. The three statements below refer to the fission process.

I   Fission may be spontaneous.

II   Fission can be produced when neutrons bombard a nucleus, which has a large mass number.

III When fission occurs, a nucleus with a large mass number may split into nuclei with smaller mass numbers, along with several neutrons.

Which statement(s) is/are true?

A   III only

B   I and II only

C   I and III only

D   II and III only

E   I, II and III

[Turn over

SECTION B

Write your answers to questions 31 to 37 in the answer book.

31. A spectator at A walks to C, the opposite corner of a playing field, by walking from A to B and then from B to C as shown in the diagram below.

    The distance from A to B is 50 m. The distance from B to C is 150 m.

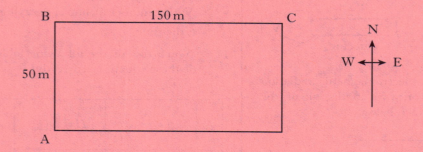

    By scale drawing or otherwise, find the resultant displacement. Magnitude and direction are required.   2

32. A football of mass 0·42 kg is thrown at a stationary student of mass 50·0 kg who is wearing roller blades, as shown in the diagram below. When the student catches the moving ball she moves to the right.

    The instantaneous speed immediately after she catches the ball is 0·10 m s^{-1}.

    Calculate the speed of the ball just before it is caught.   2

Marks

33. Calculate the size of the current in the ammeter in the circuit below. The battery has negligible internal resistance.

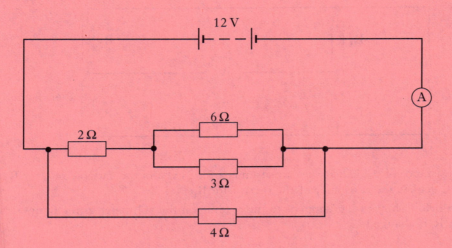

3

[Turn over

Marks

34. The Wheatstone bridge shown below is balanced.

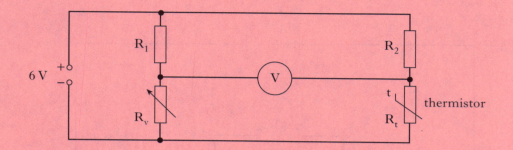

(a) R_1 has a resistance of $3 \cdot 3 \, k\Omega$, R_2 has a resistance of $2 \cdot 2 \, k\Omega$ and the variable resistor R_v is set at $225 \, \Omega$. Calculate the resistance of the thermistor R_t.

(b) The graph below shows what happens to the reading on the voltmeter as the temperature of thermistor R_t is changed.

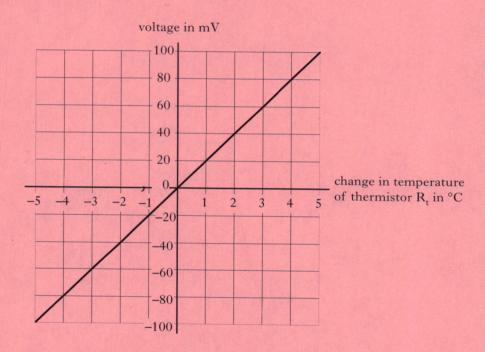

The bridge was initially balanced at 20 °C.

The temperature of R_t is increased until the reading on the voltmeter is 80 mV. What is the new temperature of the thermistor R_t?

3

35. The minimum energy required to cause an electron to be emitted from a clean zinc surface is $6 \cdot 9 \times 10^{-19} \, J$.

(a) Calculate the maximum wavelength of electromagnetic radiation which will cause an electron to be emitted from the clean zinc surface.

(b) What would be the effect of irradiating a clean zinc surface with radiation of wavelength $4 \cdot 0 \times 10^{-7} \, m$? You must justify your answer.

4

Marks

36. The diagram shows a simplified view of a gas laser.

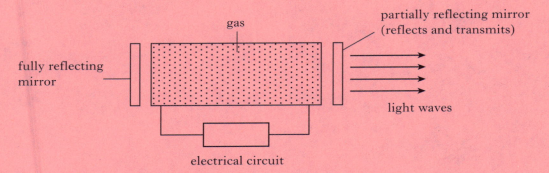

Laser stands for Light Amplification by Stimulated Emission of Radiation.

(*a*) Explain what is meant by *stimulated emission of radiation*.

(*b*) State **two** ways in which the incident radiation and the radiation it stimulates are similar.   **3**

37. A grating with 300 lines/mm is used with a spectrometer and a source of monochromatic light to view an interference pattern as shown below.

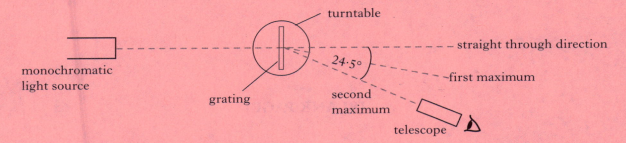

The second maximum of interference is observed when the telescope is at an angle of 24·5°.
Calculate the wavelength of the light.   **3**

[END OF QUESTION PAPER]

[BLANK PAGE]

3220/202

| SCOTTISH CERTIFICATE OF EDUCATION 1998 | FRIDAY, 15 MAY 1.00 PM – 3.30 PM | PHYSICS HIGHER GRADE Paper II |

Read carefully

1 All questions should be attempted.

2 Enter the question number clearly in the margin beside each question.

3 Any necessary data will be found in the Data Sheet on page two.

4 Care should be taken not to give an unreasonable number of significant figures in the final answers to calculations.

5 Square-ruled paper (if used) should be placed inside the front cover of the answer book for return to the Scottish Qualifications Authority.

SCOTTISH
QUALIFICATIONS
AUTHORITY

DATA SHEET
COMMON PHYSICAL QUANTITIES

Quantity	Symbol	Value	Quantity	Symbol	Value
Speed of light in vacuum	c	3.00×10^8 m s^{-1}	Mass of electron	m_e	9.11×10^{-31} kg
Charge on electron	e	-1.60×10^{-19} C	Mass of neutron	m_n	1.675×10^{-27} kg
Gravitational acceleration	g	9.8 m s^{-2}	Mass of proton	m_p	1.673×10^{-27} kg
Planck's constant	h	6.63×10^{-34} J s			

REFRACTIVE INDICES

The refractive indices refer to sodium light of wavelength 589 nm and to substances at a temperature of 273 K.

Substance	Refractive index	Substance	Refractive index
Diamond	2·42	Glycerol	1·47
Crown glass	1·50	Water	1·33
Ice	1·31	Air	1·00
Perspex	1·49		

SPECTRAL LINES

Element	Wavelength/nm	Colour	Element	Wavelength/nm	Colour
Hydrogen	656	Red	Cadmium	644	Red
	486	Blue-green		509	Green
	434	Blue-violet		480	Blue
	410	Violet			
	397	Ultraviolet			
	389	Ultraviolet			
Sodium	589	Yellow			

Lasers		
Element	Wavelength/nm	Colour
Carbon dioxide	9550 } 10590	Infrared
Helium-neon	633	Red

PROPERTIES OF SELECTED MATERIALS

Substance	Density/ kg m^{-3}	Melting Point/ K	Boiling Point/ K	Specific Heat Capacity/ J kg^{-1} K^{-1}	Specific Latent Heat of Fusion/ J kg^{-1}	Specific Latent Heat of Vaporisation/ J kg^{-1}
Aluminium	2.70×10^3	933	2623	9.02×10^2	3.95×10^5	. . . .
Copper	8.96×10^3	1357	2853	3.86×10^2	2.05×10^5	. . . .
Glass	2.60×10^3	1400	. . . .	6.70×10^2	. . . .	. . . .
Ice	9.20×10^2	273	. . . .	2.10×10^3	3.34×10^5	. . . .
Glycerol	1.26×10^3	291	563	2.43×10^3	1.81×10^5	8.30×10^5
Methanol	7.91×10^2	175	338	2.52×10^3	9.9×10^4	1.12×10^6
Sea Water	1.02×10^3	264	377	3.93×10^3	. . . .	. . . .
Water	1.00×10^3	273	373	4.19×10^3	3.34×10^5	2.26×10^6
Air	1·29	. . . .	. . . .	. . . .	. . . .	. . . .
Hydrogen	9.0×10^{-2}	14	20	1.43×10^4	. . . .	4.50×10^5
Nitrogen	1·25	63	77	1.04×10^3	. . . .	2.00×10^5
Oxygen	1·43	55	90	9.18×10^2	. . . .	2.40×10^5

The gas densities refer to a temperature of 273 K and a pressure of 1.01×10^5 Pa.

Marks

1. A trolley of mass 2·0 kg is catapulted up a slope. The slope is at an angle of 20° to the horizontal as shown in the diagram below. The speed of the trolley when it loses contact with the catapult is 3·0 m s^{-1}.

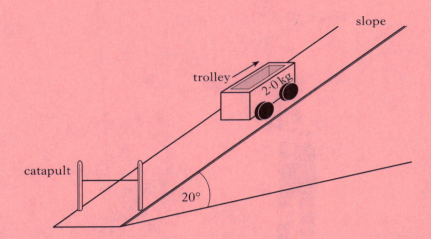

The size of the force of friction acting on the trolley as it moves up the slope is 1·3 N.

(a) (i) Calculate the component of the weight of the trolley acting parallel to the slope.

  (ii) Draw a diagram to show the forces acting on the trolley as it moves **up the slope** and is no longer in contact with the catapult.

  Show only forces or components of forces acting parallel to the slope. Name the forces.

  (iii) Show that, as the trolley moves up the slope, it has a deceleration of magnitude 4·0 m s^{-2}.

  (iv) Calculate the time taken for the trolley to reach its furthest point up the slope.

  (v) Calculate the maximum distance the trolley travels along the slope.   9

The trolley now moves back down the slope.

(b) (i) Draw a diagram to show the forces acting on the trolley as it moves **down the slope**. Show only forces or components of forces acting parallel to the slope. Name the forces.

  (ii) The magnitude of the deceleration of the trolley is 4·0 m s^{-2} as it moves up the slope. Explain why the magnitude of the acceleration is not 4·0 m s^{-2} when the trolley moves down the slope.   2

          (11)

[Turn over

Marks

2. A student performs an experiment to study the motion of the school lift as it moves upwards.

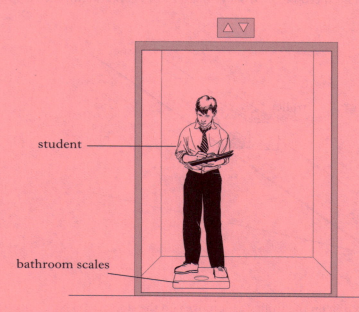

The student stands on bathroom scales during the lift's journey upwards.

The student records the reading on the scales at different parts of the lift's journey as follows.

Part of journey	*Reading on scales*
At the start (while the lift is accelerating)	678 N
In the middle (while the lift is moving at a steady speed)	588 N
At the end (while the lift is decelerating)	498 N

(a) Show that the mass of the student is 60 kg.   2

(b) Calculate the initial acceleration of the lift.   2

(c) Calculate the deceleration of the lift.   1

(d) During the journey, the lift accelerates for 1·0 s, moves at a steady speed for 3·0 s and decelerates for a further 1·0 s before coming to rest.

Sketch the acceleration-time graph for this journey.   2

(7)

Marks

3. The apparatus in the diagram is being used to investigate the average force exerted by a golf club on a ball.

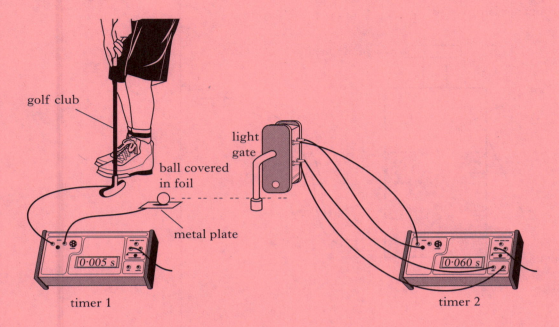

The club hits the stationary ball. Timer 1 records the time of contact between the club and the ball. Timer 2 records the time taken for the ball to pass through the light gate beam.

The mass of the ball is $45\cdot00 \pm 0\cdot01$ g.

The time of the contact between club and ball is $0\cdot005 \pm 0\cdot001$ s.

The time for the ball to pass through the light gate beam is $0\cdot060 \pm 0\cdot001$ s.

The diameter of the ball is 24 ± 1 mm.

(*a*) (i) Calculate the speed of the ball as it passes through the light gate.

    (ii) Calculate the average force exerted on the ball by the golf club.　　　　　**3**

(*b*) (i) Show by calculation which measurement contributes the largest percentage error in the final value of the average force on the ball.

    (ii) Express your numerical answer to (*a*)(ii) in the form

       final value ± absolute error.　　　　　**3**

(6)

[Turn over

Marks

4. The rigid container of a garden sprayer has a total volume of 8·0 litres (8×10^{-3} m³).

A gardener pours 5·0 litres (5×10^{-3} m³) of water into the container. The pressure of the air inside the container is $1·01 \times 10^{5}$ Pa.

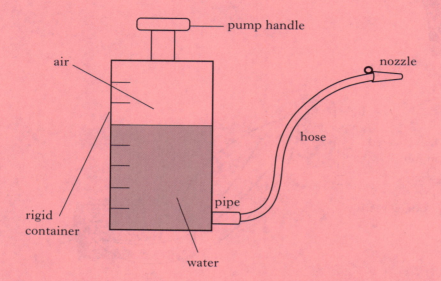

(a) Calculate the mass of air in the sprayer. Use information from the data sheet.   **3**

(b) The gardener now pumps air into the container until the pressure of the air inside it becomes $3·0 \times 10^{5}$ Pa.

   (i) The area of the water surface in contact with the compressed air is $7·0 \times 10^{-3}$ m². Calculate the force which the compressed air exerts on the water.

   (ii) Water is now released through the nozzle. Calculate the final pressure of the air inside the sprayer when the volume of water falls from 5·0 litres (5×10^{-3} m³) to 2·0 litres (2×10^{-3} m³).

     Assume the temperature of the compressed air remains constant.

    4

    (7)

Marks

5. (*a*)   A cell of e.m.f. 1·5 V and internal resistance 0·75 Ω is connected as shown in the following circuit.

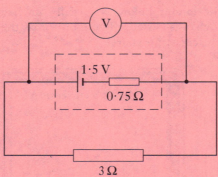

   (i)   Calculate the value of the reading on the voltmeter.

   (ii) What is the value of the "lost volts" in this circuit?   **5**

(*b*)   A battery of e.m.f. 6 V and internal resistance, *r*, is connected to a variable resistor R as shown in the following circuit diagram.

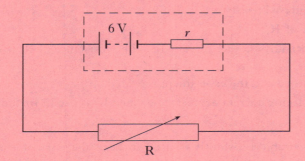

The graph below shows how the "lost volts" of this battery changes as the resistance of R increases.

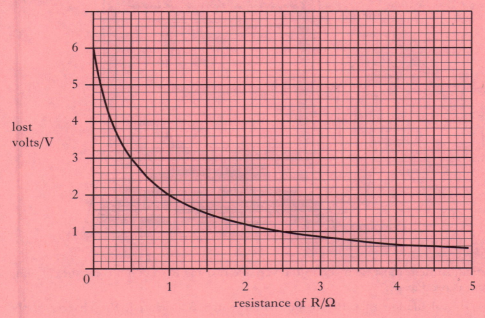

   (i)   Use information from the graph to calculate the p.d. across the terminals of the battery (t.p.d.) when the resistance of R is 1 Ω.

   (ii) Calculate the internal resistance, *r*, of the battery.   **4**

                                                                    (9)

Marks

6. (*a*) A capacitor has a value of 5 μF. Explain in terms of electric charge what this means.   **1**

(*b*) The 5 μF capacitor shown in the circuit below is initially uncharged. The circuit is connected to a computer and switch S is closed. The monitor of the computer displays a graph of current against time as the capacitor charges.

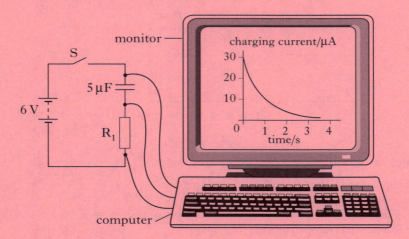

The battery has negligible internal resistance.

  (i) Calculate the resistance of R_1.

  (ii) The resistor R_1 is replaced by another resistor R_2. The resistance of R_2 is half that of R_1.

  The capacitor is discharged and the experiment repeated.

  Sketch the graph of charging current against time when R_2 is used. Include values on the axes.   **3**

(*c*) In the following circuit a variable resistor R is used to keep the current constant as a different capacitor charges. The graphs on the monitor show how the charging current and p.d. across the capacitor vary with time after switch S is closed.

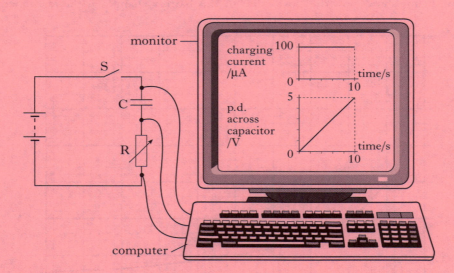

  (i) What adjustment must be made to the variable resistor R so that a constant charging current is produced?

  (ii) Show by calculation that 10 seconds after switch S is closed, the charge on the capacitor is 1mC.

  (iii) Calculate the capacitance of C.   **4**

(8)

Marks

7. The diagram below shows a cathode ray tube used in an oscilloscope.

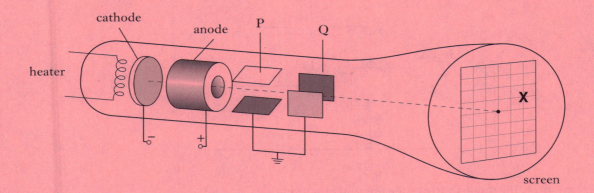

The electrons which are emitted from the cathode start from rest and reach the anode with a speed of $4 \cdot 2 \times 10^7 \, \mathrm{m \, s^{-1}}$.

(a)   (i) Calculate the kinetic energy in joules of each electron just before it reaches the anode.

     (ii) Calculate the p.d. between the anode and the cathode.   4

(b)   Describe how the spot at the centre of the screen produced by the electrons can be moved to position **X**.

    Your answer must make reference to the relative sizes and polarity (signs) of the voltages applied to plates P and Q.   2

                                                                 (6)

[Turn over

Marks

8. An op-amp is connected in an amplifier circuit as shown below.

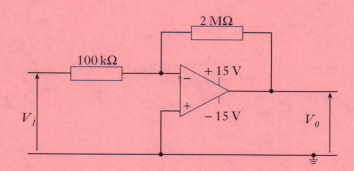

(a) (i) State the mode in which the op-amp is working.

(ii) Calculate the gain of this amplifier circuit.

(iii) The following graph shows how the input voltage V_1 varies with time.

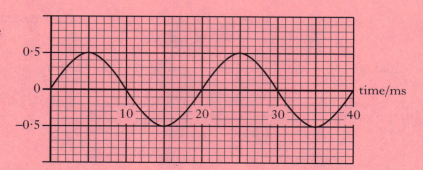

Sketch a graph to show how the output voltage V_0 varies with time.   **5**

(b) The amplifier circuit above is modified to give the following output voltage.

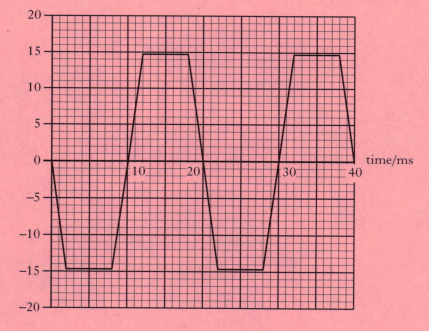

(i) Explain the shape of the output voltage graph between 2 ms and 8 ms.

(ii) Describe **two** alterations which could be made to the circuit above to give this output voltage.   **3**

(8)

Marks

9. The line emission spectrum of hydrogen has four lines in the visible spectrum as shown in the following diagram.

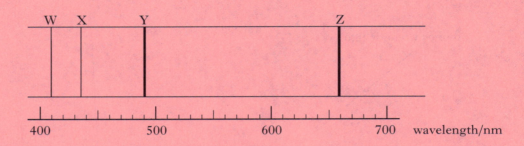

These four lines are caused by electron transitions in a hydrogen atom from high energy levels to a low energy level E_2 as shown below.

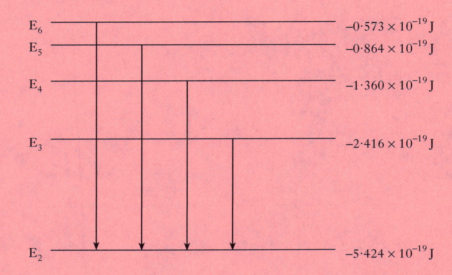

(a) From the information above, state which spectral line W, X, Y or Z is produced by an electron transition from E_3 to E_2.

1

(b) Explain why lines Y and Z in the line emission spectrum are brighter than the other two lines.

1

(c) Infrared radiation of frequency 7.48×10^{13} Hz is emitted from a hydrogen atom.

(i) Calculate the energy of one photon of this radiation.

(ii) Show by calculation which electron transition produces this radiation.

4

(6)

[Turn over

Marks

10. (*a*) The following diagram shows a ray of monochromatic light passing from air into a block of borate glass.

The diagram is drawn to scale.

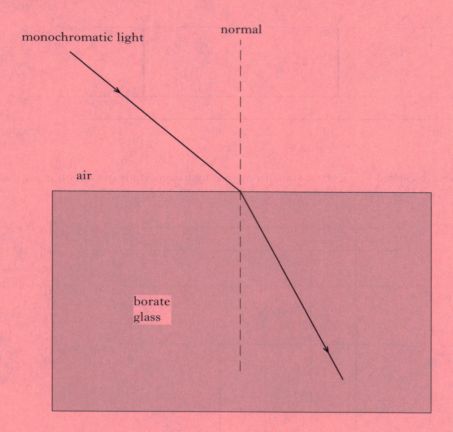

(i) Use measurements taken from the above diagram to calculate the refractive index of borate glass for this light. You will need to use a protractor.

(ii) Calculate the value of the critical angle for this light in the borate glass.   **4**

Marks

10. **(continued)**

   (b) The following graph shows how refractive index depends on the type of material and the wavelength in air of the light used.

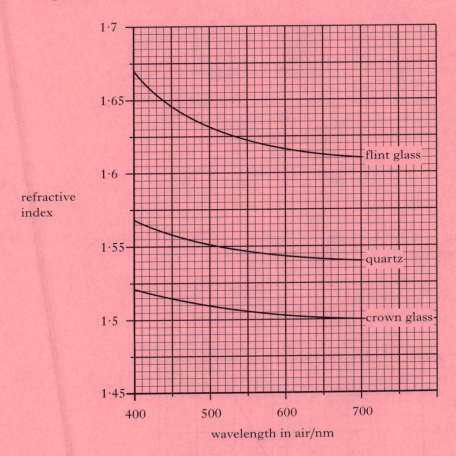

A ray of light of wavelength 510 nm in air passes into a block of quartz.

   (i) Calculate the wavelength of this light in the quartz.

   (ii) Explain what happens to the value of the critical angle in quartz as the wavelength of visible light increases.

   (iii) A ray of white light enters a triangular prism made of crown glass, producing a visible spectrum on a screen, as shown below.

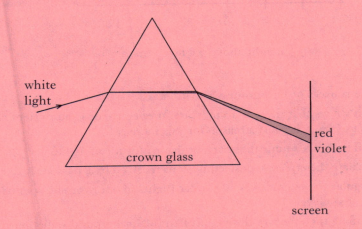

The crown glass prism is now replaced by a similar prism made from flint glass.

Describe how the visible spectrum on the screen will be different from before.

5

(9)

Marks

11. (*a*)   The first three stages in a radioactive decay series are shown below.

$$^{238}_{92}U \longrightarrow ^{234}_{90}Th \longrightarrow ^{234}_{91}Pa \longrightarrow ^{234}_{92}U$$

(i)   What particle is emitted when Thorium (Th) decays to Protactinium (Pa)?

(ii) How many neutrons are in the nuclide represented by $^{238}_{92}U$?

(iii) In the next stage of the above decay series, an alpha particle is emitted.

Copy and complete this stage of the radioactivity decay series shown below, giving values for a, b, c and d, and naming the element X.

$$^{234}_{92}U \longrightarrow ^{a}_{b}X + ^{c}_{d}\alpha$$

5

(*b*)   The following graph shows how the effective dose equivalent rate due to background radiation varies with height above sea level.

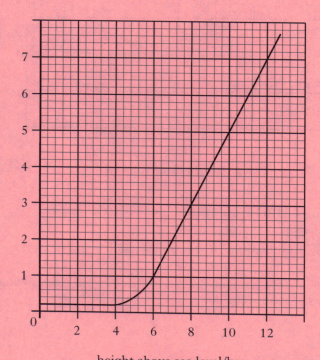

height above sea level/km

(i)   Name **two** sources of background radiation.

(ii) The graph shows that there is an increase in effective dose equivalent rate at altitudes greater than 4 km. Suggest a reason for this increase.

(iii) An aircraft makes a 7 hour flight at a cruising altitude of 10 km.

(A) Calculate the effective dose equivalent received by a passenger during this flight.

(B) A regular traveller makes 40 similar flights in one year and spends the rest of the year at sea level.

Calculate the effective dose equivalent of background radiation received by this traveller in that year.

8

(13)

[END OF QUESTION PAPER]

[BLANK PAGE]

[BLANK PAGE]

3220/201

SCOTTISH CERTIFICATE OF EDUCATION 1999	FRIDAY, 14 MAY 9.00 AM – 10.30 AM	PHYSICS HIGHER GRADE Paper I

Read Carefully

1 All questions should be attempted.

2 The following data should be used when required unless otherwise stated.

Speed of light in vacuum c	$3 \cdot 00 \times 10^{8}$ m s^{-1}	Planck's constant h	$6 \cdot 63 \times 10^{-34}$ J s
Charge on electron e	$-1 \cdot 60 \times 10^{-19}$ C	Mass of electron m_e	$9 \cdot 11 \times 10^{-31}$ kg
Acceleration due to gravity g	$9 \cdot 8$ m s^{-2}	Mass of proton m_p	$1 \cdot 67 \times 10^{-27}$ kg

Section A (questions 1 to 30)

3 Check that the answer sheet is for Physics Higher I (Section A).

4 Answer the questions numbered 1 to 30 on the answer sheet provided.

5 Fill in the details required on the answer sheet.

6 Rough working, if required, should be done only on this question paper, or on the first two pages of the answer book provided—**not** on the answer sheet.

7 For each of the questions 1 to 30 there is only **one** correct answer and each is worth 1 mark.

8 Instructions as to how to record your answers to questions 1–30 are given on page two.

Section B (questions 31 to 37)

9 Answer questions numbered 31 to 37 in the answer book provided.

10 Fill in the details on the front of the answer book.

11 Enter the question number clearly in the margin of the answer book beside each of your answers to questions 31 to 37.

12 Care should be taken **not** to give an unreasonable number of significant figures in the final answers to calculations.

SCOTTISH
QUALIFICATIONS
AUTHORITY

SECTION A

For questions 1 to 30 in this section of the paper, an answer is recorded on the answer sheet by indicating the choice A, B, C, D or E by a stroke made in ink in the appropriate box of the answer sheet—see the example below.

EXAMPLE

The energy unit measured by the electricity meter in your home is the

    A ampere

    B kilowatt-hour

    C watt

    D coulomb

    E volt.

The correct answer to the question is B—kilowatt-hour. Record your answer by drawing a heavy vertical line joining the two dots in the appropriate box on your answer sheet in the column of boxes headed B. The entry on your answer sheet would now look like this:

If after you have recorded your answer you decide that you have made an error and wish to make a change, you should cancel the original answer and put a vertical stroke in the box you now consider to be correct. Thus, if you want to change an answer D to an answer B, your answer sheet would look like this:

If you want to change back to an answer which has already been scored out, you should enter a tick (✓) to the RIGHT of the box of your choice, thus:

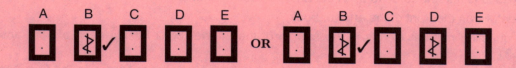

SECTION A

Answer questions 1–30 on the answer sheet.

1. A long-distance athlete runs from point P to point Q and then jogs to point R.

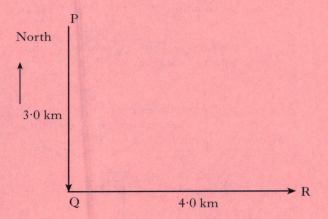

She takes 20 minutes to run from P to Q and then a further 40 minutes to jog from Q to R.

Which row in the following table correctly gives her average speed and her average velocity for the whole journey from P to R?

	Average speed	Average velocity
A	$7 \cdot 0 \ km \, h^{-1}$	$5 \cdot 0 \ km \, h^{-1}$ on a bearing of 143°
B	$7 \cdot 0 \ km \, h^{-1}$	$7 \cdot 0 \ km \, h^{-1}$ on a bearing of 127°
C	$7 \cdot 0 \ km \, h^{-1}$	$5 \cdot 0 \ km \, h^{-1}$ on a bearing of 127°
D	$5 \cdot 0 \ km \, h^{-1}$	$7 \cdot 0 \ km \, h^{-1}$ on a bearing of 127°
E	$5 \cdot 0 \ km \, h^{-1}$	$5 \cdot 0 \ km \, h^{-1}$ on a bearing of 143°

2. The velocity-time graph for an object travelling along a straight line is shown below.

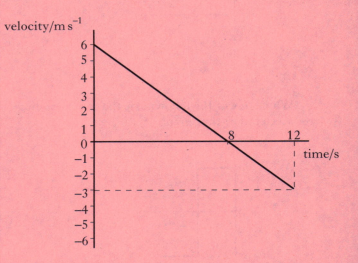

The displacement of the object during the first 12 seconds is

A   18 m

B   24 m

C   30 m

D   36 m

E   54 m.

[Turn over

3. The velocity-time graph for an object travelling in a straight line is shown below.

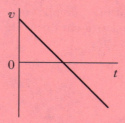

Which one of the following is the corresponding acceleration-time graph?

A
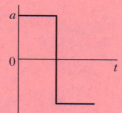

B
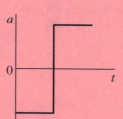

C
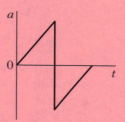

D
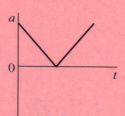

E
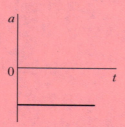

4. In the equation $s = ut + \frac{1}{2}at^2$ for an object moving in a straight line with a uniform acceleration "a", the term "ut" represents

A   the initial velocity of the object

B   the initial acceleration of the object

C   the velocity of the object after t seconds

D   the acceleration of the object after t seconds

E   the displacement of the object after t seconds if the acceleration is zero.

5. A motorcycle stunt involves crossing a ravine from P to Q. The motorcycle is travelling horizontally when it leaves point P.

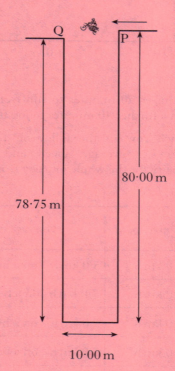

Neglecting air resistance and taking the acceleration due to gravity to be $10\,\mathrm{m\,s^{-2}}$, the time taken to cross the ravine from P to Q is

A $0.125\,\mathrm{s}$

B $0.25\,\mathrm{s}$

C $0.5\,\mathrm{s}$

D $1.0\,\mathrm{s}$

E $4.0\,\mathrm{s}$.

6. A crane on an oil-rig is used to raise a sunken buoy from the seabed. The weight of the buoy is 4900 N and the buoyancy force (upthrust) acting on it is 1000 N. When the buoy is being raised vertically at a constant speed, a force of 800 N acts on it due to water resistance.

What is the size of the force which the vertical cable applies to the buoy?

A   200 N

B   1800 N

C   3100 N

D   4700 N

E   6700 N

7. The graph below shows how the force, F, exerted on an object varies with time t.

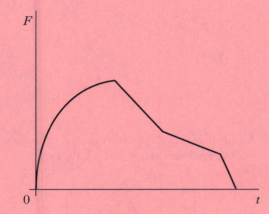

The area under the graph represents the object's change of

A   acceleration

B   velocity

C   momentum

D   kinetic energy

E   potential energy.

8. A spacecraft of mass 1200 kg has landed on a planet where the gravitational field strength is 5 N kg^{-1}. The spacecraft rests on three pads, each of contact area 0·5 m^2. The pressure exerted by these three pads on the surface of the planet is

A $8·0 \times 10^2$ Pa

B $4·0 \times 10^3$ Pa

C $7·8 \times 10^3$ Pa

D $9·0 \times 10^3$ Pa

E $1·2 \times 10^4$ Pa.

9. A girl wrote the following statements in her physics notebook.

  I   The pressure of a fixed mass of gas varies inversely as its volume, provided the temperature of the gas remains constant.

  II The pressure of a fixed mass of gas varies directly as its kelvin temperature, provided the volume of the gas remains constant.

  III A temperature **change** of 20 °C in a gas is the same as a temperature **change** of 293 K.

Which of the above statements is/are correct?

A   I only

B   II only

C   III only

D   I and II only

E   II and III only

10. On a cold morning, a motorist checks the pressure of the air in one of her car tyres. It is found to be $3·0 \times 10^5$ Pa at a temperature of 2 °C.

After a long run on a motorway, the temperature of the air in the tyre rises to 57 °C. The volume of the air in the tyre remains constant and no air escapes.

Which row in the following table gives the correct value of the final pressure of the air in the tyre and a correct statement about the final density of the air in the tyre compared to the initial density?

	Final pressure of air	Final density of air
A	$8·6 \times 10^6$ Pa	greater
B	$8·6 \times 10^6$ Pa	same
C	$8·6 \times 10^6$ Pa	less
D	$3·6 \times 10^5$ Pa	same
E	$3·6 \times 10^5$ Pa	less

[Turn over

11. A pupil is given three resistors of values $2 \cdot 0\,\Omega$, $3 \cdot 0\,\Omega$ and $6 \cdot 0\,\Omega$.

She is told to connect **all three** resistors together.

What are the values of the smallest possible resistance and the largest possible resistance which she could obtain by connecting all three resistors?

	Smallest resistance/Ω	Largest resistance/Ω
A	1·0	36·0
B	1·0	11·0
C	2·0	36·0
D	2·0	11·0
E	4·0	36·0

12. In the following circuit, the battery has an e.m.f. of 6 V and negligible internal resistance.

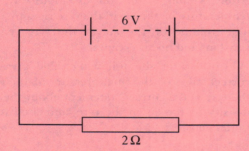

The energy required to move one coulomb of charge round this circuit is

A   3 J

B   6 J

C   12 J

D   18 J

E   72 J.

13. When the potential difference across a heater of resistance R ohms is V volts, there is a current of I amperes in the heater.

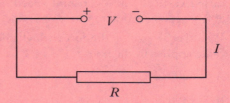

The power of the heater, in watts, is given by

A IR

B $\dfrac{V^2}{R}$

C $\dfrac{V}{I}$

D $V^2 R$

E IR^2.

14. A pupil sets up the following circuit to measure the internal resistance r of a battery.

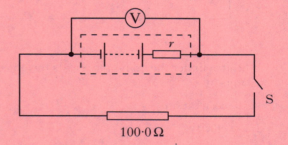

The reading on the voltmeter is $12 \cdot 0\,V$ when switch S is open. The reading drops to $10 \cdot 0\,V$ when switch S is closed.

The internal resistance of the battery is

A $0 \cdot 00\,\Omega$

B $0 \cdot 05\,\Omega$

C $16 \cdot 7\,\Omega$

D $20 \cdot 0\,\Omega$

E $100 \cdot 0\,\Omega$.

15. A balanced Wheatstone bridge circuit is set up as shown.

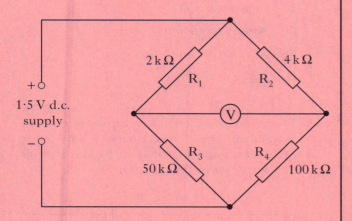

Which of the following changes will cause the Wheatstone bridge to be changed to an out-of-balance condition?

I   Doubling the value of R_1 and doubling the value of R_2

II   Doubling the value of R_1 and doubling the value of R_4

III   Doubling the voltage of the supply

A   I only

B   II only

C   I and II only

D   II and III only

E   I, II and III

16. An alternating voltage produces a trace on an oscilloscope screen as shown in Figure 1. The boxes on the screen measure 1 cm × 1 cm.

The time-base setting of the oscilloscope is 50 milliseconds per centimetre.

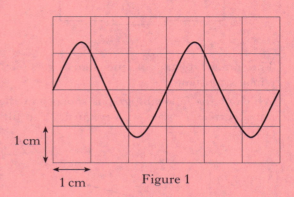

Figure 1

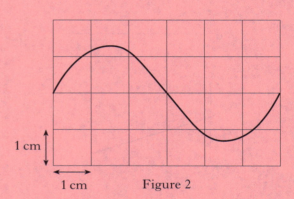

Figure 2

How should the oscilloscope controls be adjusted to change the trace on the screen to that shown in Figure 2?

	Y-amplification	Time-base setting (in ms per cm)
A	increased	100
B	unchanged	100
C	unchanged	25
D	increased	50
E	decreased	25

[Turn over

17. A resistor is connected across a signal generator, as shown below.

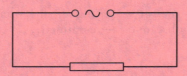

The r.m.s. voltage of the signal generator remains constant.

Which of the following graphs shows how the r.m.s. current I varies with frequency f in this circuit?

A

B

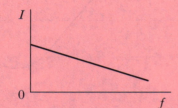

C

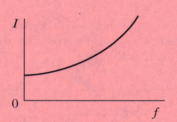

D

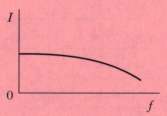

E

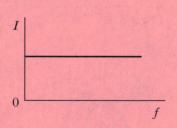

18. The farad is equivalent to the

A   volt per coulomb

B   ampere per volt

C   joule per coulomb

D   coulomb per volt

E   coulomb per joule.

19. In the following circuit, a capacitor is being charged up from a d.c. supply. The graph shows how the charge on the capacitor depends on the p.d. across the capacitor.

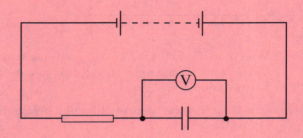

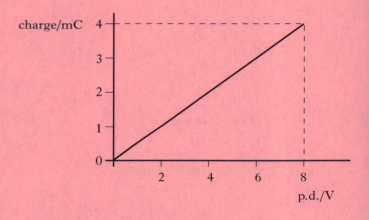

The energy stored in the capacitor when the p.d. across it is 8 V is

A   0·25 mJ

B   0·5 mJ

C   16 mJ

D   32 mJ

E   128 mJ.

20. The following operational amplifier circuit is set up.

Supply voltages of +9 V and −9 V are used for the op-amp.

The input voltage V_i is adjusted so that it rises steadily from 0 V to 6 V in 3 seconds, as shown in the graph.

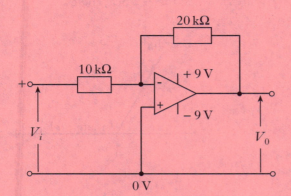

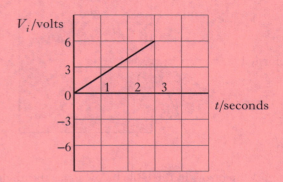

Which of the following graphs shows the correct variation of output voltage V_0 against time?

A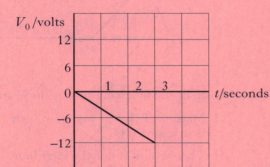

B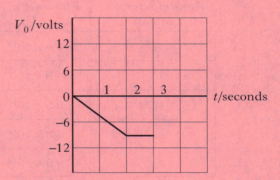

C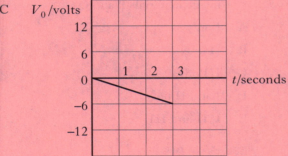

D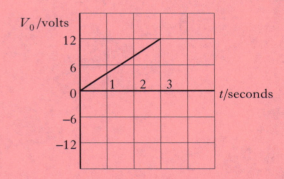

E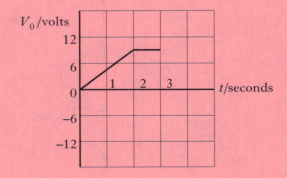

[Turn over

21. A ray of monochromatic light of frequency $6\cdot0 \times 10^{14}$ Hz in air is incident upon a block of glass of refractive index $1\cdot5$, as shown below.

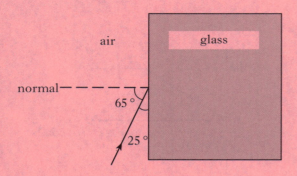

Which row in the table below gives the angle of refraction and the frequency of the light in the block of glass?

	Angle of refraction in glass	Frequency in glass/ Hz
A	$37°$	$6\cdot0 \times 10^{14}$
B	$37°$	$4\cdot0 \times 10^{14}$
C	$16°$	$6\cdot0 \times 10^{14}$
D	$16°$	$4\cdot0 \times 10^{14}$
E	$37°$	$9\cdot0 \times 10^{14}$

22. A student uses a beam of laser light to investigate critical angle. He uses two semicircular blocks made from different transparent materials, P and Q. In the following diagrams, the incident rays of light are shown at their critical angles.

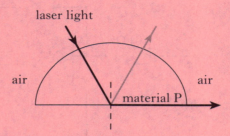

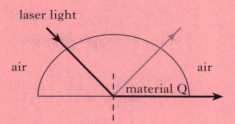

Which of the following statements is/are true?

  I Material P has a higher refractive index than material Q.

  II The wavelength of the laser light is longer inside material P than inside material Q.

  III The laser light travels at the same speed inside materials P and Q.

A   I only

B   II only

C   III only

D   I and II only

E   I, II and III

23. Microwaves with a wavelength of 3 cm in air are sent towards two slits in a metal sheet, as shown below.

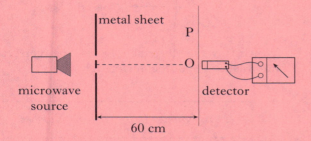

With the detector at a distance of 60 cm from the metal sheet, a position of maximum intensity is obtained at the central position O.

The detector is moved up from position O until the next maximum is obtained at position P.

A second microwave source with a different wavelength then replaces the first source. It produces its first MINIMUM at position P.

The wavelength of the second microwave source is

A   1·5 cm

B   2·5 cm

C   4·5 cm

D   6·0 cm

E   20·0 cm.

24. Which row in the following table gives the approximate wavelengths of red, green and blue light in nanometres?

	Red light/nm	Green light/nm	Blue light/nm
A	700	550	480
B	700	480	550
C	900	700	550
D	700	550	300
E	480	550	700

25. In the following passage, three words have been replaced by the letters X, Y and Z.

"The intensity of light incident on a surface is equal to the X per square metre. The intensity is Y proportional to the square of the distance from a point source of light, which means that, if the distance from the source is Z, the new intensity is a quarter of the initial value."

Which of the following gives the correct words for X, Y and Z?

	X	Y	Z
A	energy	directly	doubled
B	energy	inversely	doubled
C	power	directly	quartered
D	power	inversely	doubled
E	power	inversely	quadrupled

26. Ultraviolet radiation is incident on a zinc plate. Photoelectrons with a certain maximum kinetic energy are released from the zinc. The intensity of the ultraviolet radiation is now increased.

What happens to the maximum kinetic energy of the photoelectrons and the rate at which they are released?

	Maximum kinetic energy of the photoelectrons	Rate at which photoelectrons are released
A	increases	increases
B	decreases	increases
C	increases	remains the same
D	remains the same	increases
E	remains the same	remains the same

[Turn over

27. The minimum energy required to eject an electron from a certain metal is $3 \cdot 0 \times 10^{-19}$ J. Light of frequency $4 \cdot 8 \times 10^{14}$ Hz is incident on this metal.

Which of the following statements is correct?

A   Electrons will not be ejected from the metal.

B   Electrons will be ejected with 0 J of kinetic energy.

C   Electrons will be ejected with $1 \cdot 8 \times 10^{-20}$ J of kinetic energy.

D   Electrons will be ejected with $3 \cdot 2 \times 10^{-19}$ J of kinetic energy.

E   Electrons will be ejected with $6 \cdot 2 \times 10^{-19}$ J of kinetic energy.

28. Part of the energy level diagram for a certain atom is shown below.

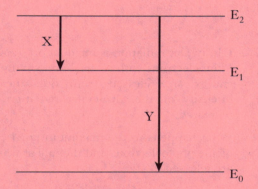

A student makes the following statements.

I Photons of higher frequency will be emitted during transition Y than during transition X.

II Photons of longer wavelength will be emitted during transition X than during transition Y.

III When an electron is in the lowest energy level, the atom is ionised.

Which of the above statements is/are true?

A   I only

B   I and II only

C   I and III only

D   II and III only

E   I, II and III

29. In a nuclear reactor, Uranium 239 decays into nuclide X by emitting a beta particle, as shown in the following reaction.

$$^{239}_{92}\text{U} \longrightarrow \text{X} + \beta$$

Which row in the table gives the correct information about the nuclide X?

	Mass Number	Atomic Number
A	235	90
B	238	92
C	239	92
D	239	93
E	239	91

30. During an experiment to measure the specific heat capacity of a liquid, the relationship $V I t = c m \Delta T$ is used.

The following quantities are measured.

$V = 12 \cdot 0 \pm 0 \cdot 1$ V

$I = 4 \cdot 2 \pm 0 \cdot 1$ A

$t = 300 \pm 1$ s

$m = 500 \pm 2$ g

$\Delta T = 15 \pm 1$ °C

Which quantity will contribute the largest uncertainty to the final answer for the specific heat capacity, c?

A   Voltage

B   Current

C   Time

D   Mass

E   Temperature change

SECTION B

Write your answers to questions 31 to 37 in the answer book.

Marks

31. A ball is rolled up a slope so that it is travelling at 14 m s^{-1} as it leaves the end of the slope.

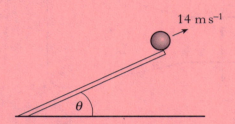

(a) The slope is set so that the angle to the horizontal, θ, is $30\,^{\circ}$.

Calculate the vertical component of the velocity of the ball as it leaves the slope.

(b) The slope is now tilted so that the angle to the horizontal, θ, is increased. The ball is rolled so that it still leaves the end of the slope at 14 m s^{-1}.

Describe and explain what happens to the maximum height reached by the ball.   3

32. Gas is often stored in cylinders at high pressure. The pressure of the gas must be reduced by a reduction valve before the gas can be used.

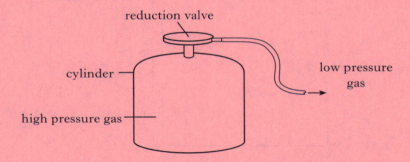

The pressure of the gas in the cylinder is $20 \times 10^5 \text{ Pa}$. The pressure of the gas as it leaves the reduction valve is $4 \times 10^5 \text{ Pa}$.

Gas with a volume of $0{\cdot}01 \text{ m}^3$ enters the reduction valve from the cylinder. What is the volume of this gas when it leaves the reduction valve, assuming that the temperature of the gas does not change?   2

[Turn over

Marks

33. The diagram shows an arrangement which is used to accelerate electrons.
The potential difference between the cathode and the anode is 2·5 kV.

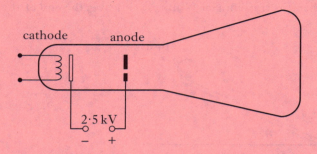

Assuming that the electrons start from rest at the cathode, calculate the speed of an electron just as it reaches the anode.

3

34. A 1·8 kΩ resistor and a variable resistor, R, are connected to a 6 volt d.c. supply as shown. The supply has negligible internal resistance. A voltmeter is used to measure the potential difference across the 1·8 kΩ resistor.

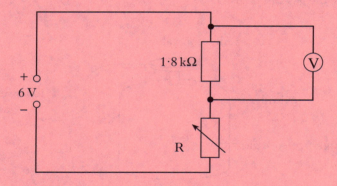

(a) Calculate the potential difference across the 1·8 kΩ resistor when the variable resistor, R, has a value of 1·2 kΩ.

(b) The resistance of the variable resistor, R, is increased. Explain why the reading on the voltmeter decreases.

3

Marks

35. (*a*) A light meter is used to measure the intensity of light from a small lamp.

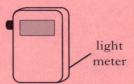
light
meter

At a distance of 1·5 m from the lamp, the intensity of the light is 0·60 W m^{-2}. What is the intensity at a distance of 4·5 m from the lamp?

(*b*) At a distance of 1·5 m from a laser, the intensity of the laser light is 400 W m^{-2}.

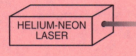
HELIUM-NEON
LASER

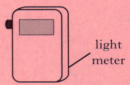
light
meter

What is the intensity of the laser light at a distance of 4·5 m from the laser? Justify your answer.   **4**

36. Energy is released from stars as a result of nuclear reactions.

One of these reactions is represented by the statement given below.

$$^{14}_{7}\text{N} + {}^{4}_{2}\text{He} \longrightarrow {}^{18}_{9}\text{F} + \text{gamma radiation}$$

(*a*) What type of nuclear reaction is described by this statement?

(*b*) Explain why this reaction results in the release of energy. You should make reference to an equation in your explanation.   **3**

37. When introducing optoelectronics to a class, a Physics teacher writes:

"One of the important factors affecting *photoelectric emission* from a metal is the *threshold frequency* for the metal".

Explain the meaning of the terms:

(*a*) photoelectric emission;

(*b*) threshold frequency.   **2**

[*END OF QUESTION PAPER*]

[BLANK PAGE]

3220/202

| SCOTTISH CERTIFICATE OF EDUCATION 1999 | FRIDAY, 14 MAY 1.00 PM – 3.30 PM | PHYSICS HIGHER GRADE Paper II |

Read carefully

1 All questions should be attempted.

2 Enter the question number clearly in the margin beside each question.

3 Any necessary data will be found in the Data Sheet on page two.

4 Care should be taken not to give an unreasonable number of significant figures in the final answers to calculations.

5 Square-ruled paper (if used) should be placed inside the front cover of the answer book for return to the Scottish Qualifications Authority.

DATA SHEET
COMMON PHYSICAL QUANTITIES

Quantity	Symbol	Value	Quantity	Symbol	Value
Speed of light in vacuum	c	$3\cdot00 \times 10^8\,\text{m s}^{-1}$	Mass of electron	m_e	$9\cdot11 \times 10^{-31}\,\text{kg}$
Charge on electron	e	$-1\cdot60 \times 10^{-19}\,\text{C}$	Mass of neutron	m_n	$1\cdot675 \times 10^{-27}\,\text{kg}$
Gravitational acceleration	g	$9\cdot8\,\text{m s}^{-2}$	Mass of proton	m_p	$1\cdot673 \times 10^{-27}\,\text{kg}$
Planck's constant	h	$6\cdot63 \times 10^{-34}\,\text{J s}$			

REFRACTIVE INDICES
The refractive indices refer to sodium light of wavelength 589 nm and to substances at a temperature of 273 K.

Substance	Refractive index	Substance	Refractive index
Diamond	2·42	Glycerol	1·47
Crown glass	1·50	Water	1·33
Ice	1·31	Air	1·00
Perspex	1·49		

SPECTRAL LINES

Element	Wavelength/nm	Colour	Element	Wavelength/nm	Colour
Hydrogen	656	Red	Cadmium	644	Red
	486	Blue-green		509	Green
	434	Blue-violet		480	Blue
	410	Violet			
	397	Ultraviolet			
	389	Ultraviolet			
Sodium	589	Yellow			

Lasers		
Element	Wavelength/nm	Colour
Carbon dioxide	9550 } 10590 }	Infrared
Helium-neon	633	Red

PROPERTIES OF SELECTED MATERIALS

Substance	Density/ kg m^{-3}	Melting Point/ K	Boiling Point/ K	Specific Heat Capacity/ J kg^{-1} K^{-1}	Specific Latent Heat of Fusion/ J kg^{-1}	Specific Latent Heat of Vaporisation/ J kg^{-1}
Aluminium	$2\cdot70 \times 10^3$	933	2623	$9\cdot02 \times 10^2$	$3\cdot95 \times 10^5$	. . . .
Copper	$8\cdot96 \times 10^3$	1357	2853	$3\cdot86 \times 10^2$	$2\cdot05 \times 10^5$	. . . .
Glass	$2\cdot60 \times 10^3$	1400	. . . .	$6\cdot70 \times 10^2$	. . . .	. . . .
Ice	$9\cdot20 \times 10^2$	273	. . . .	$2\cdot10 \times 10^3$	$3\cdot34 \times 10^5$	. . . .
Glycerol	$1\cdot26 \times 10^3$	291	563	$2\cdot43 \times 10^3$	$1\cdot81 \times 10^5$	$8\cdot30 \times 10^5$
Methanol	$7\cdot91 \times 10^2$	175	338	$2\cdot52 \times 10^3$	$9\cdot9 \times 10^4$	$1\cdot12 \times 10^6$
Sea Water	$1\cdot02 \times 10^3$	264	377	$3\cdot93 \times 10^3$	. . . .	. . . .
Water	$1\cdot00 \times 10^3$	273	373	$4\cdot19 \times 10^3$	$3\cdot34 \times 10^5$	$2\cdot26 \times 10^6$
Air	1·29	. . . .	. . . .	. . . .	. . . .	. . . .
Hydrogen	$9\cdot0 \times 10^{-2}$	14	20	$1\cdot43 \times 10^4$	. . . .	$4\cdot50 \times 10^5$
Nitrogen	1·25	63	77	$1\cdot04 \times 10^3$	. . . .	$2\cdot00 \times 10^5$
Oxygen	1·43	55	90	$9\cdot18 \times 10^2$	. . . .	$2\cdot40 \times 10^5$

The gas densities refer to a temperature of 273 K and a pressure of $1\cdot01 \times 10^5$ Pa.

Marks

1. (a) A sports car is being tested along a straight track.

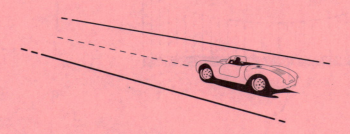

   (i) In the first test, the car starts from rest and has a constant acceleration of $4 \cdot 0 \text{ m s}^{-2}$ in a straight line for $7 \cdot 0$ seconds.

        Calculate the distance the car travels in the $7 \cdot 0$ seconds.

   (ii) In a second test, the car again starts from rest and accelerates at $4 \cdot 0 \text{ m s}^{-2}$ over twice the distance covered in the first test.

        What is the **increase** in the final speed of the car at the end of the second test compared with the final speed at the end of the first test?

   (iii) In a third test, the car reaches a speed of 40 m s^{-1}. It then decelerates at $2 \cdot 5 \text{ m s}^{-2}$ until it comes to rest.

        Calculate the distance travelled by the car while it decelerates to rest.   7

(b) A student measures the acceleration of a trolley as it moves freely down a sloping track.

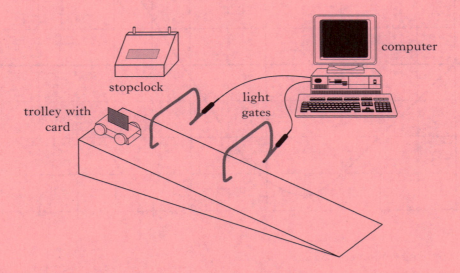

   The trolley has a card mounted on it. As it moves down the track the card cuts off the light at each of the light gates in turn. Both the light gates are connected to the computer which is used for timing.

   The student uses a stopclock to measure the time it takes the trolley to move from the first light gate to the second light gate.

   (i) List all the **measurements** that have to be made by the student and the computer to allow the acceleration of the trolley to be calculated.

   (ii) Explain fully how each of these measurements is used in calculating the acceleration of the trolley as it moves down the slope.   3

                                                                                                      (10)

Marks

2. A bungee jumper is attached to a high bridge by a thick elastic rope as shown.

The graph shows how the velocity of the bungee jumper varies with time during the first 6 seconds of a jump.

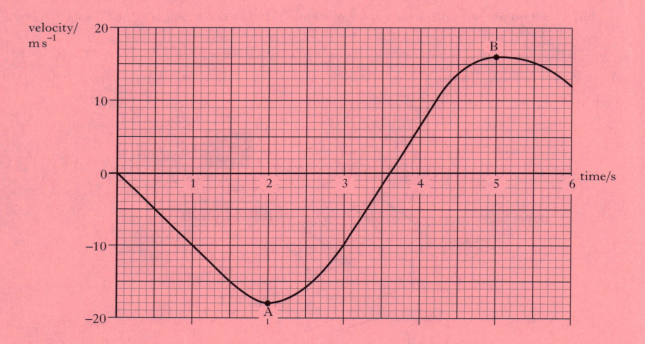

The mass of the bungee jumper is 55 kg.

(a) Using the information on the graph, state the time at which the bungee rope is at its maximum length. Justify your answer.

2

(b) Calculate the average unbalanced force, in newtons, acting on the bungee jumper between the points A and B on the graph.

2

(c) Explain, in terms of the force of the rope on the bungee jumper, why an elastic rope is used rather than a rope that cannot stretch very much.

2

(6)

Marks

3. (a) State the law of conservation of linear momentum.

1

(b) The diagram shows a linear air track on which two vehicles are free to move. Vehicle A moves towards vehicle B which is initially at rest.

A computer displays the speeds of the two vehicles before and after the collision.

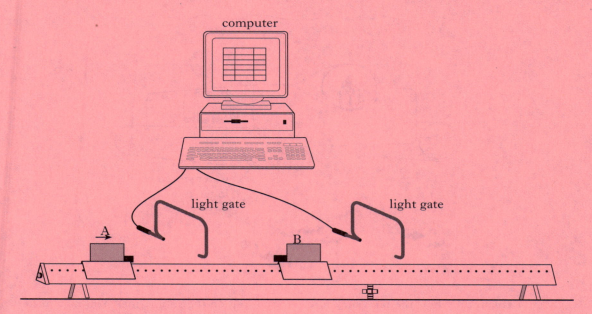

The table of results below shows the mass and velocity of each vehicle before and after the collision.

Vehicle	Mass	Velocity before collision	Velocity after collision
A	0·75 kg	0·82 m s^{-1} to the right	0·40 m s^{-1} to the right
B	0·50 kg	0·00 m s^{-1}	0·63 m s^{-1} to the right

(i) Use these results to show that the change in momentum of vehicle A is equal in size but opposite in direction to the change in momentum of vehicle B.

(ii) Use the data in the table to show whether the collision is elastic or inelastic.

5

(6)

[Turn over

4. (*a*)   Sketch a graph which shows how the pressure caused by a liquid depends on the depth below the surface of the liquid. Numerical values are not required but the axes should be clearly labelled.

1

(*b*)   There is a buoyancy (upthrust) force on a submarine when it is submerged in sea water.

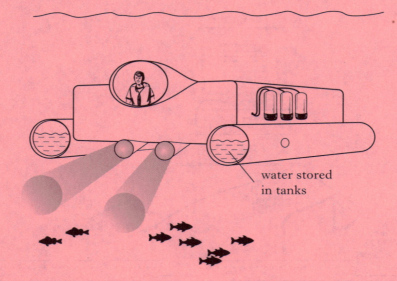

water stored
in tanks

(i)   Explain fully how the buoyancy force is produced on the submarine. You may make reference to your graph from (*a*).

(ii)   The total volume of sea water displaced by the submarine is 14·5 m³.

Calculate the mass of sea water displaced by the submarine.

(iii)   The submarine changes depth by altering the mass of water stored in tanks in the submarine.

Compressed air replaces some water in the tanks.

escaping
water

air replaces
water in tanks

Explain, in terms of the forces acting on the submarine, why replacing water in the tanks with compressed air causes the submarine to accelerate upwards.

7

(8)

Marks

5. A pupil uses a Wheatstone bridge to investigate how the resistance of a thermistor is affected by its temperature. The circuit is shown below.

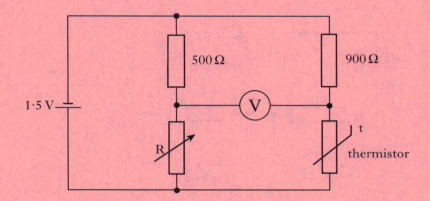

(a) The thermistor is placed in water at a temperature of 20°C and the resistance of the variable resistor, R, is adjusted to 450 Ω to balance the bridge.

Calculate the resistance of the thermistor at this temperature.   2

(b) Several pupils use the circuit to find the resistance of the thermistor when the water temperature is 30 °C. The values they obtain are as follows.

      852 Ω   854 Ω   848 Ω   851 Ω   853 Ω

Calculate:

(i) the mean of the values;

(ii) the random error in the mean.   3

(c) Their teacher says that there may have been a *systematic error* in the investigation. Describe what is meant by a *systematic error*.   1

                                                            (6)

[Turn over

Marks

6. The circuit below includes a cell with an e.m.f. of 1·60 V and internal resistance *r*.   1

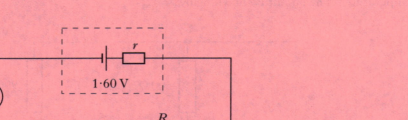

The following readings are taken from the meters.

reading on the ammeter   = 0·04 A
reading on the voltmeter V_1 = 1·20 V
reading on the voltmeter V_2 = 0·30 V

(a) Calculate the value of the lost volts in the circuit.   1

(b) Calculate the internal resistance, *r*, of the cell.   2

(c) (i) The resistance of the variable resistor is altered so that the reading on the ammeter is 0·02 A. What is the resistance of the variable resistor now?

(ii) The resistance, *R*, of the variable resistor is now decreased. What effect has this on the terminal potential difference, V_{tpd}, of the cell? You must justify your answer.   5

(8)

Marks

7. A capacitor is connected across a variable frequency supply as shown in the circuit below. The output of the supply has constant amplitude.

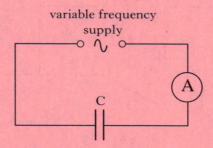

(a) (i) At a certain frequency, the current in the circuit is 200 mA r.m.s. Calculate the value of the peak current in the circuit.

(ii) The frequency of the output from the supply is now slowly increased. Sketch the graph of current against frequency for this circuit. Numerical values are not required but the axes should be clearly labelled.   3

(b) An uncharged capacitor and a resistor are connected across a 12 V d.c. supply with negligible internal resistance as shown below.

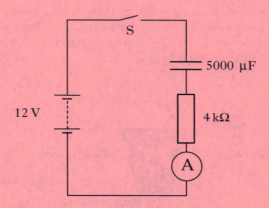

(i) The switch, S, is now closed and the capacitor charges. What charge is stored on the capacitor when the reading on the ammeter is 2 mA?

(ii) The capacitor is allowed to become fully charged. Calculate the energy now stored in the capacitor.   5

                                                                                            (8)

[Turn over

Marks

8. (*a*)   An op-amp is connected in a circuit as shown below.

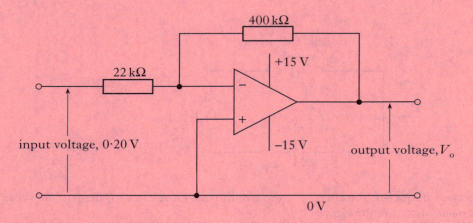

   (i)   Calculate the output voltage, V_o, when the input voltage is 0·20 V.

  (ii)   The 400 kΩ resistor develops a fault and its resistance increases to 10 MΩ. Describe
the effect this has on the output voltage.   **3**

(*b*)   A paint manufacturer needs to make sure all paint of the same type has the same reflective
properties.

The reflective property of a sample of paint is tested using a circuit that includes
photosensors. A photosensor is a device which contains a light source and a light sensor.
Light from the light source in the photosensor is reflected from the sample of paint into the
light sensor as shown in the diagram below.

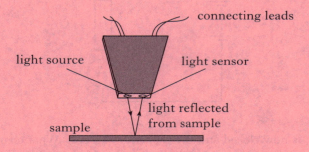

The light sensor produces an output voltage that is directly proportional to the intensity of
the light that is reflected from the paint.

Marks

8. (b) (continued)

The circuit used to test the paint includes an op-amp and two photosensors. The circuit is used first of all with a standard sample placed under **both** photosensors as shown below.

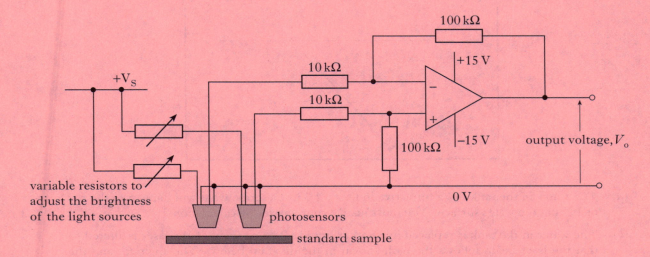

(i)   In what mode is this op-amp operating?

(ii) A technician adjusts the variable resistors until the light sources are equally bright. How will the technician know from the circuit when this has been achieved?

(iii) A sample of the paint under test and the standard sample are now placed under the photosensors as shown below.

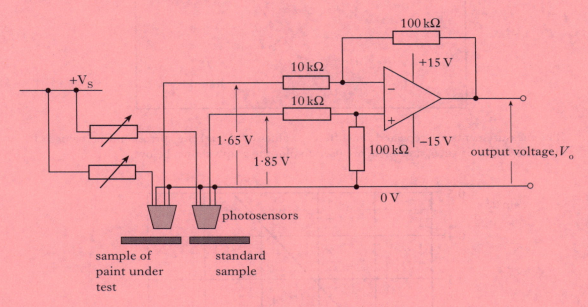

The voltage inputs from the photosensors to the op-amp circuit are:

inverting input   1·65 V;

non-inverting input   1·85 V.

Calculate the value of the output voltage V_o.

(iv) The sample of paint under test is replaced by another slightly more reflective sample. This change causes the voltage from the photosensor above the new sample to increase. State and explain the effect on the output voltage, V_o, from the op-amp.

6

(9)

Marks

9. A laser beam is used to investigate the refraction of light from water into air.

A waterproof laser is placed within a tank of water and the laser beam is directed towards the water surface as shown below.

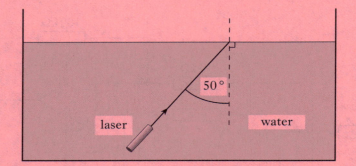

(a) The water in the tank has a refractive index of 1·33. Describe what will happen to the ray of light at the water surface. You must justify your answer by calculation.   **3**

(b) The water in the tank is replaced by another liquid. The position of the laser is altered so that the laser beam follows the path shown in the diagram below. The angle θ_1, and the angle θ_2, as shown in the diagram, are measured.

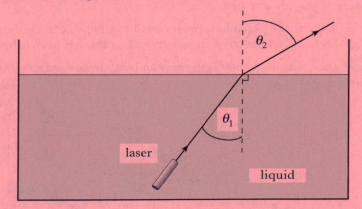

The measurements are repeated for different values of θ_1 and the corresponding values of θ_2. The values of $\sin \theta_1$ and $\sin \theta_2$ are used to plot the graph shown below.

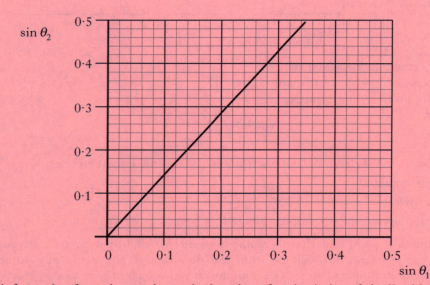

Use information from the graph to calculate the refractive index of the liquid.   **2**

(c) Light from the laser has a wavelength of 670×10^{-9} m in air. What is the wavelength of the laser light when passing through a liquid which has a refractive index of 1·47?   **2**

(7)

Marks

10. Light from a laser is shone onto a grating. The separation of the slits on the grating is 5.0×10^{-6} m. A pattern is produced on a screen as shown below.

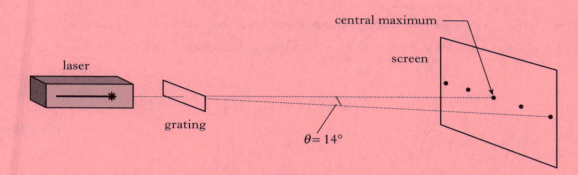

(a) (i) The angle θ between the central maximum and the 2nd order maximum is 14°.
Calculate the wavelength of the light produced by this laser.

(ii) A pupil suggests that a more accurate value for the wavelength of the laser light can be found if a grating with a slit separation of 2.0×10^{-6} m is used. Explain why this suggestion is correct.   4

(b) The laser is replaced by a source of white light and the pattern on the screen changes to a white central maximum with other maxima in the form of continuous **spectra** on each side of the central maximum.

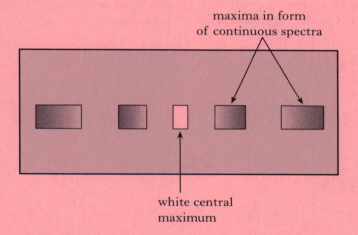

Explain:

(i) why the central maximum is white;

(ii) why the other maxima are in the form of continuous spectra.   2

                                                                                  (6)

[Turn over

Marks

11. (*a*) A sample of pure semiconductor material has a small amount of impurity atoms added to form a p-type semiconductor.

    (i) What is this process called?

    (ii) How does the addition of the impurity atoms affect the resistance of the material?   **2**

(*b*) A p-n junction is used as a photodiode and a voltage is applied across it as shown below.

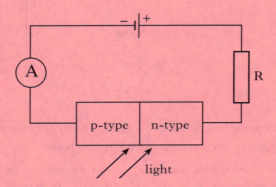

    (i) In what mode is the photodiode operating?

    (ii) The intensity of the light at the junction of the photodiode increases. Describe and explain what happens to the current in the circuit.   **3**

(*c*) The sensitivity of a certain photodiode is greatest when each incident photon has an energy of $2 \cdot 3 \times 10^{-19}$ J. Calculate the wavelength of these photons.   **3**

            (8)

Marks

12. (*a*)   The radiology department in a hospital uses radioactive iodine to examine the functioning
of the thyroid gland in a patient. Radioactive iodine is produced by a nuclear reaction
when the nuclei of Tellurium atoms absorb neutrons.

The statement for this reaction is shown below.

$$^{130}_{52}\text{Te} + {}^{1}_{0}\text{n} \longrightarrow {}^{131}_{53}\text{I} + \text{radiation}$$

State the type of radiation emitted in this reaction.   **1**

(*b*)   The thyroid gland of the patient receives an absorbed dose of 750 μGy of radiation from
the radioactive iodine.

  (i)   Calculate the total energy absorbed if the gland has a mass of 0·04 kg.

  (ii) The average dose equivalent rate for the gland is 12·5 μSv h^{-1}. The radioactive iodine
is present in the gland of the patient for 120 hours. What is the quality factor of the
radiation?   **5**

(*c*)   A source of gamma radiation is stored inside a cabinet in a room where background
radiation is negligible. The count rate outside the cabinet is 1200 counts per minute.

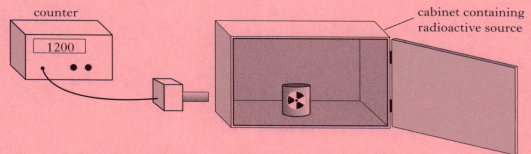

The cabinet is now lined with lead 24 mm thick. The lead has a half-value thickness of
8 mm for the radiation.

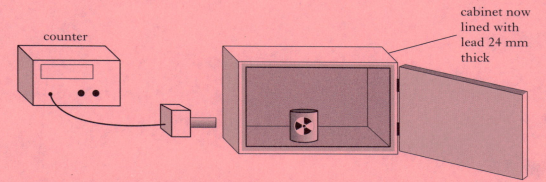

What is the new count rate outside the cabinet?   **2**

                                                                                 (8)

[*END OF QUESTION PAPER*]

[BLANK PAGE]

[C069/SQP031]

Higher

Physics

Specimen Question Paper

Time: 2 hours 30 minutes

NATIONAL
QUALIFICATIONS

Read Carefully

1 All questions should be attempted.

Section A (questions 1 to 20)

2 Check that the answer sheet is for Higher Physics (Section A).

3 Answer the questions numbered 1 to 20 on the answer sheet provided.

4 Fill in the details required on the answer sheet.

5 Rough working, if required, should be done only on this question paper, or on the first two pages of the answer book provided—**not** on the answer sheet.

6 For each of the questions 1 to 20 there is only **one** correct answer and each is worth 1 mark.

7 Instructions as to how to record your answers to questions 1–20 are given on page three.

Section B (questions 21 to 29)

8 Answer questions numbered 21 to 29 in the answer book provided.

9 Fill in the details on the front of the answer book.

10 Enter the question number clearly in the margin of the answer book beside each of your answers to questions 21 to 29.

11 Care should be taken **not** to give an unreasonable number of significant figures in the final answers to calculations.

SCOTTISH
QUALIFICATIONS
AUTHORITY

DATA SHEET
COMMON PHYSICAL QUANTITIES

Quantity	Symbol	Value	Quantity	Symbol	Value
Speed of light in vacuum	c	3.00×10^8 m s^{-1}	Mass of electron	m_e	9.11×10^{-31} kg
Charge on electron	e	-1.60×10^{-19} C	Mass of neutron	m_n	1.675×10^{-27} kg
Gravitational acceleration	g	9.8 m s^{-2}	Mass of proton	m_p	1.673×10^{-27} kg
Planck's constant	h	6.63×10^{-34} J s			

REFRACTIVE INDICES
The refractive indices refer to sodium light of wavelength 589 nm and to substances at a temperature of 273 K.

Substance	Refractive index	Substance	Refractive index
Diamond	2·42	Water	1·33
Crown glass	1·50	Air	1·00

SPECTRAL LINES

Element	Wavelength/nm	Colour	Element	Wavelength/nm	Colour
Hydrogen	656	Red	Cadmium	644	Red
	486	Blue-green		509	Green
	434	Blue-violet		480	Blue
	410	Violet		Lasers	
	397	Ultraviolet	Element	Wavelength/nm	Colour
	389	Ultraviolet	Carbon dioxide	9550 } 10590 }	Infrared
Sodium	589	Yellow	Helium-neon	633	Red

PROPERTIES OF SELECTED MATERIALS

Substance	Density/ kg m^{-3}	Melting Point/ K	Boiling Point/ K
Aluminium	2.70×10^3	933	2623
Copper	8.96×10^3	1357	2853
Ice	9.20×10^2	273	. . . .
Sea Water	1.02×10^3	264	377
Water	1.00×10^3	273	373
Air	1·29	. . . .	. . . .
Hydrogen	9.0×10^{-2}	14	20

The gas densities refer to a temperature of 273 K and a pressure of 1.01×10^5 Pa.

SECTION A

For questions 1 to 20 in this section of the paper, an answer is recorded on the answer sheet by indicating the choice A, B, C, D or E by a stroke made in ink in the appropriate box of the answer sheet—see the example below.

EXAMPLE

The energy unit measured by the electricity meter in your home is the

    A ampere

    B kilowatt-hour

    C watt

    D coulomb

    E volt.

The correct answer to the question is B—kilowatt-hour. Record your answer by drawing a heavy vertical line joining the two dots in the appropriate box on your answer sheet in the column of boxes headed B. The entry on your answer sheet would now look like this:

If after you have recorded your answer you decide that you have made an error and wish to make a change, you should cancel the original answer and put a vertical stroke in the box you now consider to be correct. Thus, if you want to change an answer D to an answer B, your answer sheet would look like this:

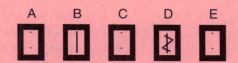

If you want to change back to an answer which has already been scored out, you should enter a tick (✓) to the RIGHT of the box of your choice, thus:

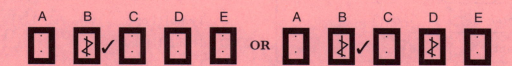

SECTION A

Answer questions 1–20 on the answer sheet.

1. A student sets up the apparatus in the diagram to measure the average acceleration of a model car as it travels between P and Q.

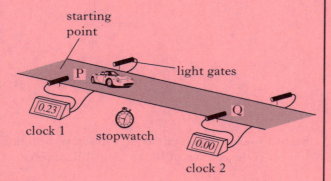

For one run, the following measurements were recorded along with their estimated uncertainty.

clock 1 reading $= 0.23\,s \pm 0.01\,s$
clock 2 reading $= 0.12\,s \pm 0.01\,s$
stopwatch reading $= 0.95\,s \pm 0.20\,s$
length of car $= 0.050\,m \pm 0.002\,m$
distance PQ $= 0.30\,m \pm 0.01\,m$

The measurement which gives the largest percentage uncertainty is the

A   reading on clock 1

B   reading on clock 2

C   reading on the stopwatch

D   length of the car

E   distance PQ.

2. Which of the rows in the following table is correct?

	Scalar	Vector
A	weight	force
B	force	mass
C	mass	distance
D	distance	momentum
E	momentum	time

3. An object is projected with a velocity V at an angle θ with the horizontal.

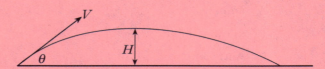

At the point of maximum height H reached by the object, the vertical acceleration and the vertical and horizontal velocities are given by

	Vertical acceleration	Vertical velocity	Horizontal velocity
A	g	0	$V \sin \theta$
B	0	$V \cos \theta$	$V \sin \theta$
C	0	0	$V \cos \theta$
D	0	$V \sin \theta$	0
E	g	0	$V \cos \theta$

4. An inelastic collision takes place between a moving object and a stationary object. Both objects have the same mass. In this situation, which of the following quantities is/are conserved for this system?

   I   Momentum

   II Total energy

   III Kinetic energy

A   III only

B   I and II only

C   I and III only

D   II and III only

E   I, II and III

5. The diagram shows two trolleys X and Y about to collide. The momentum of each trolley before impact is given.

After the collision, the trolleys travel in opposite directions.

The magnitude of the momentum of trolley X is $2\,kg\,m\,s^{-1}$.

What is the corresponding magnitude of the momentum of trolley Y in $kg\,m\,s^{-1}$?

A   6

B   8

C   10

D   30

E   34

6. A motorcycle safety helmet has a soft, thick, inner lining which is compressed on impact with the skull. This design protects the skull because it

A   decreases the impulse applied to the skull

B   increases the time of impact with the skull

C   decreases the time of impact with the skull

D   decreases the change in momentum of the skull

E   increases the change in momentum of the skull.

7. A container of cross-sectional area A contains a liquid of density ρ.

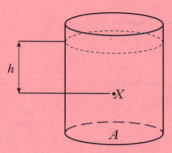

At point X, a distance h below the surface, the pressure due to the liquid is

A $\rho g/A$

B ρh

C hg/A

D $\rho h/A$

E ρhg.

8. The diagram shows an 8 V supply connected to two lamps. The supply has negligible internal resistance.

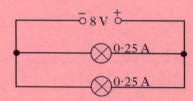

In 16 s, the total electrical energy converted in the two lamps is

A   2 J

B   4 J

C   32 J

D   48 J

E   64 J.

9. The diagram shows a circuit used to determine the e.m.f. *E* and the internal resistance *r* of a cell.

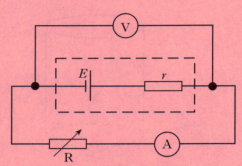

Which graph correctly shows how the potential difference *V* across the terminals of the cell varies with the current *I* in the circuit?

A

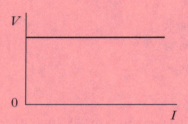

B

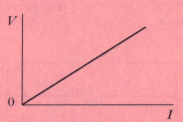

C

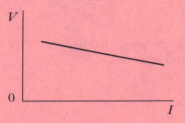

D

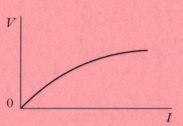

E

10. The graph represents a sinusoidal alternating voltage.

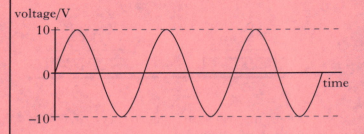

The r.m.s. (root mean square) voltage is

A   5 V

B $\dfrac{10}{\sqrt{2}}$ V

C   10 V

D $10\sqrt{2}$ V

E   20 V.

11. A resistor and an ammeter are connected to a signal generator as shown below.

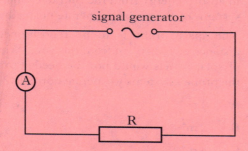

signal generator

The signal generator has an output voltage of constant amplitude and variable frequency.

Which of the following graphs shows the correct relationship between the current I in the resistor and the frequency f of the output voltage of the signal generator?

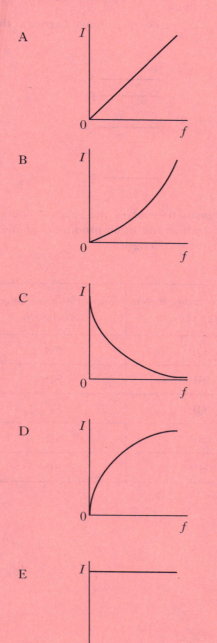

A

B

C

D

E

12. An ideal operational amplifier is connected as shown.

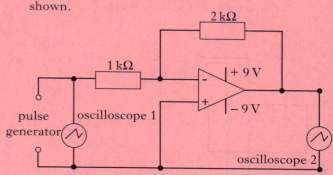

Oscilloscope 1 displays the following input signal.

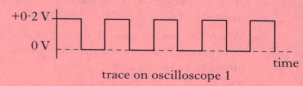

trace on oscilloscope 1

For this input signal, which output signal would be displayed by oscilloscope 2?

A

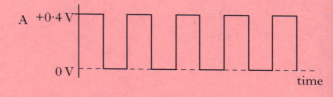

B

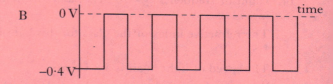

C

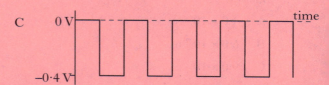

D

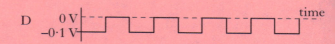

E

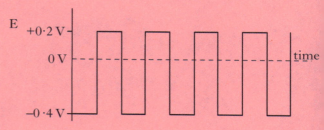

13. Two identical loudspeakers are connected to a signal generator as shown below.

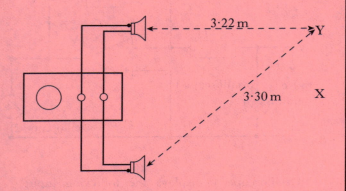

A microphone at X detects a maximum of intensity of sound.

When the microphone is moved slowly in the direction XY, it detects the first minimum of intensity of sound at Y.

The wavelength of the sound emitted from the loudspeakers is

A   0·08 m

B   0·16 m

C   0·32 m

D   0·80 m

E   1·60 m.

14. Light of frequency 5×10^{14} Hz passes from air into glass.

The refractive index of the glass for this light is 1·5.

The speed of light in air is 3×10^8 m s^{-1}.

What is the wavelength of this light in the glass?

A $4·0 \times 10^{-7}$ m

B $6·0 \times 10^{-7}$ m

C $9·0 \times 10^{-7}$ m

D $1·0 \times 10^{23}$ m

E $1·5 \times 10^{23}$ m

15. A space probe is positioned 3×10^{11} m from the Sun. It needs solar panels with an area of 4 m^2 to absorb energy from the Sun to enable all the systems of the probe to operate normally.

The space probe is to be repositioned at a distance of 6×10^{11} m from the Sun. What area of solar panels would now be needed to enable the probe's systems to operate normally?

A   1 m^2

B   2 m^2

C   4 m^2

D   8 m^2

E   16 m^2

16. The diagram represents four possible energy levels of an atom.

Electrons can make transitions between the levels.

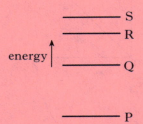

Which transition involves the greatest energy change and which transition produces radiation of the longest wavelength?

	Transition with greatest energy change	Transition with longest wavelength
A	QP	SR
B	SP	SP
C	QP	SP
D	SP	SR
E	SR	SP

17. The diagram shows the line spectrum from a hot gas. Lines X, Y and Z are associated with different electron transitions within an atom of the gas.

Red end of Spectrum			Violet end of Spectrum
	X	Y	Z

Which of the following reasons can account for the line Y appearing much brighter than lines X and Z?

A   Light causing line Y has the longest wavelength.

B   Light causing line Y has the highest frequency.

C   Light causing line Y originates in the hottest part of the gas.

D   Light causing line Y is the result of electrons making a much larger transition than those responsible for lines X and Z.

E   Light causing line Y is the result of more electrons making that particular transition than either of the other two lines.

18. Which of the following statements is/are true?

  I   In a light emitting diode, positive and negative charge carriers recombine to emit light.

 II   In a p-n junction diode, the majority charge carriers in the p-type material are electrons.

III   In a photodiode, electron-hole pairs are produced by the action of light.

A   I only

B   I and II only

C   I and III only

D   II and III only

E   I, II and III

19. In a laser, a photon is emitted when an electron makes a transition from a higher energy level to a lower one, as shown below.

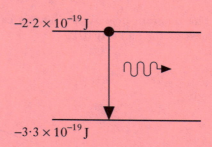

The energy in each pulse of light from the laser is 10 J. How many photons are there in each pulse?

A $\dfrac{10}{5\cdot5 \times 10^{-19}}$

B $\dfrac{10}{(1\cdot1 + 1\cdot6) \times 10^{-19}}$

C $\dfrac{10}{3\cdot3 \times 10^{-19}}$

D $\dfrac{10}{2\cdot2 \times 10^{-19}}$

E $\dfrac{10}{1\cdot1 \times 10^{-19}}$

20. Two materials X and Y are joined together and used as an absorber for a source of gamma rays.

X has a half-value thickness of 2 cm for the gamma rays.

Y has a half-value thickness of 4 cm for the gamma rays.

The intensity of the gamma rays at the left side of the absorber is I.

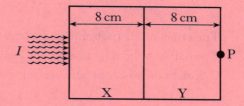

The intensity of the gamma rays at point P, on the right side of the absorber is

A $I/8$

B $I/16$

C $I/32$

D $I/64$

E $I/128$.

SECTION B

Write your answers to questions 21 to 29 in the answer book.

Marks

21. The diagram below represents a catapult about to launch a small steel ball horizontally.   The mass of the ball is 0·10 kg.

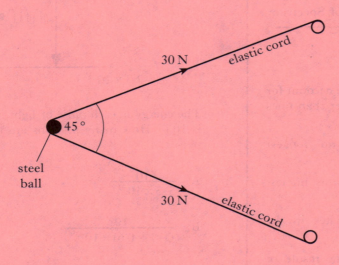

(a) Calculate

  (i) the size of the resultant force exerted by the catapult on the steel ball

  (ii) the initial acceleration of the steel ball in the horizontal direction.   **4**

(b) The steel ball is aimed at the centre of a target which is 6·0 m away.   The ball leaves the catapult travelling at 34 m s⁻¹ in a horizontal direction.

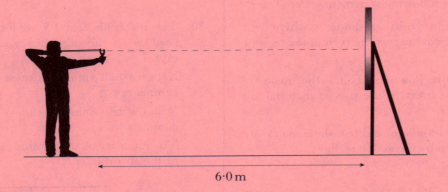

The effect of air friction may be neglected.

The ball hits the target below the centre.

Calculate the distance between the centre of the target and the point of impact.   **3**

(7)

Marks

22. A girl is playing with her sledge on a snow covered slope.
    The girl is pulled up to the top of the slope by her father.
    The combined mass of the girl and her sledge is 40 kg.

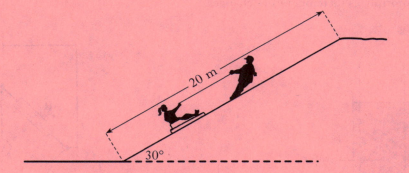

The frictional force exerted by the snow on the sledge is 120 N and can be assumed to be constant in magnitude.

(a) How much work is done **against friction** by her father when pulling the girl and sledge a distance of 20 m up the slope? — 2

(b) At the top of the slope, the girl and sledge are released from rest, and slide back down the slope.

  (i) What is the unbalanced force acting down the slope on the girl and sledge?

  (ii) Calculate the speed of the girl and sledge at the foot of the slope. — 5

(7)

Marks

23. A student carries out an investigation into the relationship between the volume and temperature of a trapped sample of air. He sets up the apparatus shown below in diagram I.

The student decides to use a temperature sensor connected as part of a Wheatstone bridge circuit, as shown in the diagram II, to measure the temperature of the water. The resistance of the sensor varies uniformly as its temperature changes.

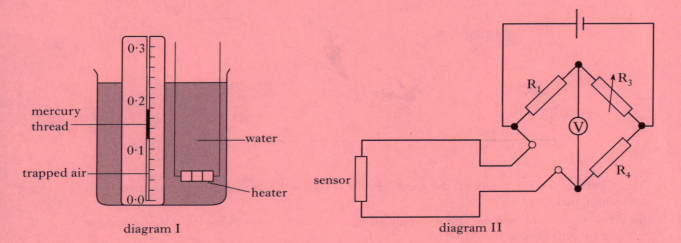

diagram I   diagram II

(a)   (i)   Explain what is meant by a **balanced** Wheatstone bridge.

    (ii)   How should the student calibrate the voltmeter as part of the bridge circuit for use as a thermometer over the range 0 °C to 100 °C. No other thermometer is available for use.   **3**

(b)   Using the apparatus shown in diagram I, the student places the temperature sensor in the beaker of water.

By heating the water, the student obtains a series of results for the volume and temperature of the trapped air.

The results are shown in the table below.

Volume/units	42	45	46	49	51
Temperature/°C	15	30	45	60	75
Temperature/K					

    (i)   Copy the above table. Complete the table, giving the temperature in kelvin.

    (ii)   Use **all** of the data from your completed table to establish the relationship between the volume and temperature of the trapped air.

    (iii)   State **two** properties of the trapped air which should be kept constant during this investigation.   **4**

                  (7)

Marks

24. The diagram illustrates a cathode ray tube used in an oscilloscope.

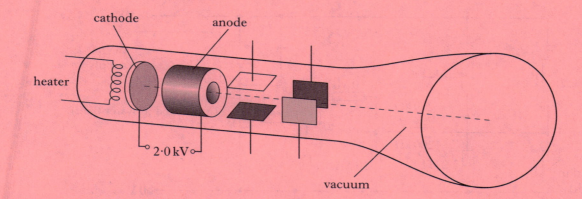

Electrons are released from the hot cathode and are accelerated uniformly by a p.d. of $2 \cdot 0$ kV between the cathode and anode. The distance between the cathode and anode is $0 \cdot 10$ m.

(*a*) Show that the amount of work done in accelerating an electron between the cathode and anode is $3 \cdot 2 \times 10^{-16}$ J.

1

(*b*) Assuming that the electrons start from rest at the cathode, calculate the speed of an electron just as it reaches the anode.

2

(*c*) (i) Show that the acceleration of an electron as it moves from the cathode to the anode is $3 \cdot 5 \times 10^{15}$ m s^{-2}.

    (ii) Calculate the time taken by an electron to travel from the cathode to the anode.

4

(*d*) The distance between the cathode and anode in the cathode ray tube is increased.

The same p.d. is applied between the cathode and anode.

Explain the effect this has on the speed of an electron just as it reaches the anode.

2

(9)

25. The diagram shows a circuit used to control the temperature in a water bath.

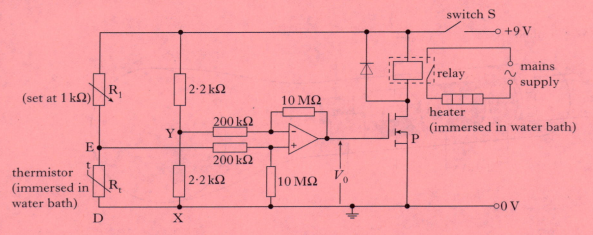

The graph below shows how the resistance of the thermistor varies with its temperature.

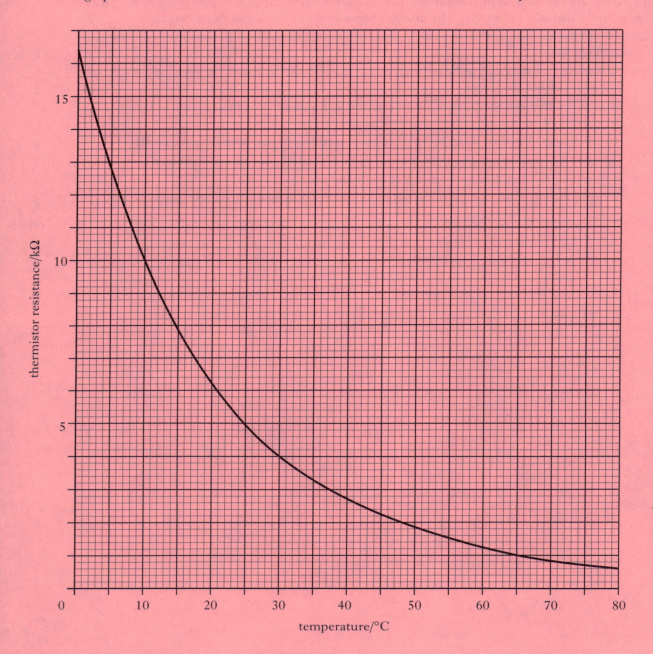

Marks

25. (continued)

Switch S is now closed. The temperature of the water in the bath is 8 °C.

(a) Calculate the potential difference across XY.   **1**

(b) Calculate the potential difference across DE.   **3**

(c) When the switch S is closed and the temperature of the water is 8 °C, the heater is switched
     on by the circuit.
     Explain fully how this happens.   **2**

(d) In the circuit diagram, what is the component whose symbol is labelled P?   **1**

                                                                                     (7)

Marks

26. A 220 µF capacitor is to be charged using the circuit shown below.

    The 12 V battery has negligible internal resistance.

    The capacitor is initially uncharged.

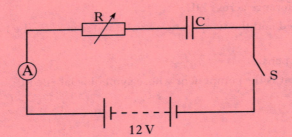

After switch S is closed, the charging current is kept constant at 20 µA by adjusting the resistance of the variable resistor, R, while the capacitor is charging.

(a) What is the initial resistance of R?   2

(b) While the capacitor is charging, should the resistance of R be increased or decreased to keep the current constant?

    Justify your answer.   2

(c) Calculate

    (i) the charge on the capacitor 45 s after the switch S is closed

    (ii) the potential difference across R at this time.   5

                                                                                                            (9)

Marks

27. (a) Describe, with the aid of a diagram, how you would use a source of monochromatic light
    and a semi-circular glass block to measure the critical angle for the light in this glass.   **2**

(b) A ray of monochromatic light is incident on the face XY of the right angled glass prism as
    shown below. The diagram is drawn to scale. The refractive index of the glass for this light
    is 1·49.

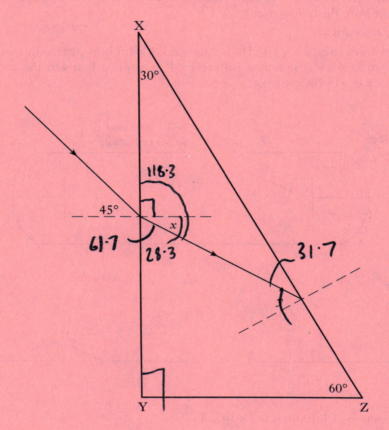

(i) Use the value given for the refractive index to calculate the size of angle *x*.
    Your working must be shown.

(ii) Using a protractor, or otherwise, find the size of angle *y*.

(iii) Calculate the critical angle for this ray of light in the glass.

(iv) Describe and explain what happens to the ray of light at face XZ.   **7**

          (9)

28. (*a*) A source of bright red light and a source of faint blue light are shone in turn on to a metal surface for the same length of time.

Light from both sources is found to eject electrons from the metal surface.

(i) Explain why the maximum kinetic energy of the electrons ejected by the faint blue light is greater than the maximum kinetic energy of the electrons ejected by the bright red light.

(ii) Will the light from the red source eject the same number of electrons every second as the light from the blue source?

Justify your answer.   **3**

(*b*) Radiation of frequency 6.8×10^{14} Hz is shone on to a lithium surface in an evacuated glass tube as shown below. A potential difference V is applied between the collector and the lithium surface by closing switch S.

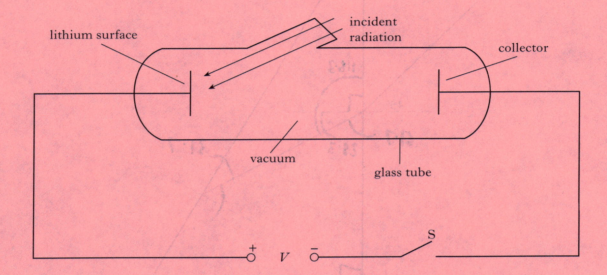

The work function of lithium is 3.7×10^{-19} J.

(i) Calculate the energy of each photon of the incident radiation.

(ii) Switch S is open.

Determine the maximum kinetic energy of an electron which is ejected from the surface of the lithium by the incident radiation.

(iii) Switch S is now closed.

Calculate the minimum value of the potential difference, V, which would prevent any photoelectrons from reaching the collector.   **5**

                                                                                        (8)

Marks

29. (*a*) One reaction which takes place in the core of a nuclear reactor is represented as follows.

$$^{235}_{92}\text{U} + {}^{1}_{0}\text{n} \longrightarrow {}^{140}_{x}\text{Ce} + {}^{94}_{40}\text{Zr} + 2{}^{1}_{0}\text{n} + 6{}^{0}_{-1}\text{e}$$

    (i)   State the name given to the above type of reaction.

   (ii)   Determine the value of x.

  (iii) Explain briefly why this reaction releases energy.   **3**

(*b*) In a test laboratory, a sample of tissue is exposed to three different radiations at the same time.

Information relating to the radiations and the absorbed dose rates for this tissue is given in the table below.

Type of radiation	Quality factor	Absorbed dose rate
Gamma	1	$1000\ \mu\text{Gy h}^{-1}$
Thermal neutrons	3	$200\ \mu\text{Gy h}^{-1}$
Fast neutrons	10	$40\ \mu\text{Gy h}^{-1}$

    (i)   Explain the meaning of "absorbed dose".

   (ii)   The sample of tissue is to receive a total dose equivalent of 50 mSv from these radiations.

Use the information given to calculate the number of hours of exposure needed for the sample of tissue to receive this required dose equivalent.   **4**

(7)

[END OF QUESTION PAPER]

[BLANK PAGE]

X069/301

NATIONAL QUALIFICATIONS 2000	WEDNESDAY, 31 MAY 9.00 AM – 11.30 AM	PHYSICS HIGHER

Read Carefully

1 All questions should be attempted.

Section A (questions 1 to 20)

2 Check that the answer sheet is for Physics Higher (Section A).

3 Answer the questions numbered 1 to 20 on the answer sheet provided.

4 Fill in the details required on the answer sheet.

5 Rough working, if required, should be done only on this question paper, or on the first two pages of the answer book provided—**not** on the answer sheet.

6 For each of the questions 1 to 20 there is only **one** correct answer and each is worth 1 mark.

7 Instructions as to how to record your answers to questions 1–20 are given on page three.

Section B (questions 21 to 29)

8 Answer questions numbered 21 to 29 in the answer book provided.

9 Fill in the details on the front of the answer book.

10 Enter the question number clearly in the margin of the answer book beside each of your answers to questions 21 to 29.

11 Care should be taken to give an appropriate number of significant figures in the final answers to calculations.

SCOTTISH QUALIFICATIONS AUTHORITY

DATA SHEET
COMMON PHYSICAL QUANTITIES

Quantity	Symbol	Value	Quantity	Symbol	Value
Speed of light in vacuum	c	$3 \cdot 00 \times 10^8$ m s^{-1}	Mass of electron	m_e	$9 \cdot 11 \times 10^{-31}$ kg
Magnitude of the charge on an electron	e	$1 \cdot 60 \times 10^{-19}$ C	Mass of neutron	m_n	$1 \cdot 675 \times 10^{-27}$ kg
Gravitational acceleration	g	$9 \cdot 8$ m s^{-2}	Mass of proton	m_p	$1 \cdot 673 \times 10^{-27}$ kg
Planck's constant	h	$6 \cdot 63 \times 10^{-34}$ J s			

REFRACTIVE INDICES
The refractive indices refer to sodium light of wavelength 589 nm and to substances at a temperature of 273 K.

Substance	Refractive index	Substance	Refractive index
Diamond	2·42	Water	1·33
Crown glass	1·50	Air	1·00

SPECTRAL LINES

Element	Wavelength/nm	Colour	Element	Wavelength/nm	Colour
Hydrogen	656	Red	Cadmium	644	Red
	486	Blue-green		509	Green
	434	Blue-violet		480	Blue
	410	Violet			
	397	Ultraviolet		*Lasers*	
	389	Ultraviolet	Element	Wavelength/nm	Colour
			Carbon dioxide	9550 ⎱ 10590 ⎰	Infrared
Sodium	589	Yellow	Helium-neon	633	Red

PROPERTIES OF SELECTED MATERIALS

Substance	Density/ kg m^{-3}	Melting Point/ K	Boiling Point/ K
Aluminium	$2 \cdot 70 \times 10^3$	933	2623
Copper	$8 \cdot 96 \times 10^3$	1357	2853
Ice	$9 \cdot 20 \times 10^2$	273	. . . .
Sea Water	$1 \cdot 02 \times 10^3$	264	377
Water	$1 \cdot 00 \times 10^3$	273	373
Air	$1 \cdot 29$	. . . .	. . . .
Hydrogen	$9 \cdot 0 \times 10^{-2}$	14	20

The gas densities refer to a temperature of 273 K and a pressure of $1 \cdot 01 \times 10^5$ Pa.

SECTION A

For questions 1 to 20 in this section of the paper, an answer is recorded on the answer sheet by indicating the choice A, B, C, D or E by a stroke made in ink in the appropriate box of the answer sheet—see the example below.

EXAMPLE

The energy unit measured by the electricity meter in your home is the

    A   ampere

    B   kilowatt-hour

    C   watt

    D   coulomb

    E   volt.

The correct answer to the question is B—kilowatt-hour. Record your answer by drawing a heavy vertical line joining the two dots in the appropriate box on your answer sheet in the column of boxes headed B. The entry on your answer sheet would now look like this:

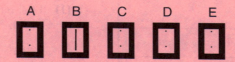

If after you have recorded your answer you decide that you have made an error and wish to make a change, you should cancel the original answer and put a vertical stroke in the box you now consider to be correct. Thus, if you want to change an answer D to an answer B, your answer sheet would look like this:

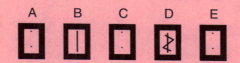

If you want to change back to an answer which has already been scored out, you should enter a tick (✓) to the RIGHT of the box of your choice, thus:

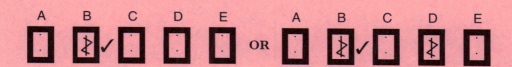

SECTION A

Answer questions 1–20 on the answer sheet.

1. Which of the following is a scalar quantity?

   A   Velocity

   B   Acceleration

   C   Mass

   D   Force

   E   Momentum

2. A woman walks 12 km due North. She then turns round immediately and walks 4 km due South. The total journey takes 4 hours.

   Which row in the following table gives the correct values for her average velocity and average speed?

	Average velocity	*Average speed*
A	4 km h⁻¹ due N	4 km h⁻¹
B	4 km h⁻¹ due N	2 km h⁻¹
C	3 km h⁻¹ due N	4 km h⁻¹
D	2 km h⁻¹ due N	4 km h⁻¹
E	2 km h⁻¹ due N	3 km h⁻¹

3. The following velocity-time graph describes the motion of a ball, dropped from rest and bouncing several times.

   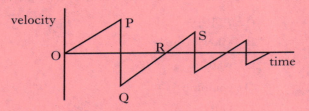

   Which of the following statements is/are true?

   I   The ball hits the ground at P.

   II   The ball is moving upwards between Q and R.

   III   The ball is moving upwards between R and S.

   A   I only

   B   II only

   C   III only

   D   I and II only

   E   I and III only

4. The momentum of a rock of mass 4 kg is 12 kg m s⁻¹.

   The kinetic energy of the rock is

   A   6 J

   B   18 J

   C   36 J

   D   144 J

   E   288 J.

5. Density is measured in

   A $N m^{-2}$

   B $N m^{-3}$

   C $kg m^{3}$

   D $kg m^{-2}$

   E $kg m^{-3}$.

6. The pressure of a fixed mass of gas is 100 kPa at a temperature of −52 °C. The volume of the gas remains constant.

   At what temperature would the pressure of the gas be 200 kPa?

   A   −26 °C

   B   +52 °C

   C   +147 °C

   D   +169 °C

   E   +442 °C

7. The end of a bicycle pump is sealed with a stopper so that the air in the chamber is trapped.

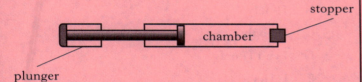

   The plunger is now pushed in slowly causing the air in the chamber to be compressed. As a result of this the pressure of the trapped air increases.

   Assuming that the temperature remains constant, which of the following explain/s why the pressure increases?

   I   The air molecules increase their average speed.

   II The air molecules are colliding more often with the walls of the chamber.

   III Each air molecule is striking the walls of the chamber with greater force.

   A   II only

   B   III only

   C   I and II only

   D   I and III only

   E   I, II and III

8. One volt is

   A   one coulomb per joule

   B   one joule coulomb

   C   one joule per coulomb

   D   one joule per second

   E   one coulomb per second.

9. In the following circuit the reading on the voltmeter is zero.

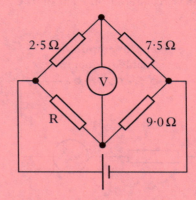

   The resistance of resistor R is

   A   0·33 Ω

   B   0·48 Ω

   C   2·1 Ω

   D   3·0 Ω

   E   27 Ω.

[Turn over

10. The circuits below have identical a.c. supplies which are set at a frequency of 200 Hz. A current is registered on each of the ammeters A_1 and A_2.

constant amplitude
variable frequency

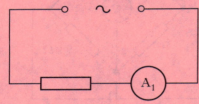

constant amplitude
variable frequency

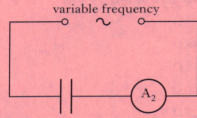

The frequency of each a.c. supply is now increased to 500 Hz.

What happens to the readings on ammeters A_1 and A_2?

		A_1	A_2
A		increases	decreases
B		decreases	increases
C		no change	no change
D		no change	decreases
E		no change	increases

11. A student makes the following statements about ideal op-amps.

  I An op-amp used in the inverting mode inverts the input signal.

  II The gain equation for the inverting mode is

$$\frac{V_o}{V_1} = -\frac{R_1}{R_f}$$

  where the symbols have their usual meanings.

  III An op-amp used in the differential mode amplifies the sum of its two input voltages.

Which of the above statements is/are correct?

A I only

B II only

C III only

D I and II only

E I, II and III

12. An op-amp circuit is connected as shown below.

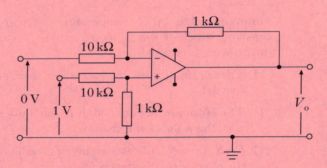

What is the value of the output voltage V_o?

A   10 V

B   0·1 V

C   0 V

D   −0·1 V

E   −10 V

13. The circuit below is used to generate square waves. The amplitude of the alternating input voltage is 6 V.

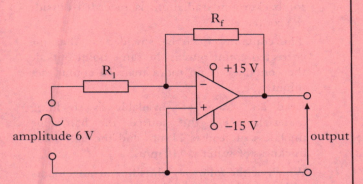

Which values for resistors R_1 and R_f will produce an approximate square wave output?

	R_1	R_f
A	$1\,k\Omega$	$10\,k\Omega$
B	$5\,k\Omega$	$10\,k\Omega$
C	$10\,k\Omega$	$10\,k\Omega$
D	$10\,k\Omega$	$5\,k\Omega$
E	$10\,k\Omega$	$1\,k\Omega$

14. Waves from coherent sources, S_1 and S_2, produce an interference pattern. Maxima of intensity are detected at the positions shown below.

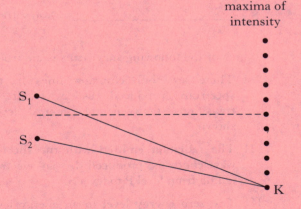

The path difference $S_1K - S_2K$ is 154 mm. The wavelength of the waves is

A 15·4 mm

B 25·7 mm

C 28·0 mm

D 30·8 mm

E 34·2 mm.

15. When white light passes through a grating, maxima of intensity are produced on a screen, as shown below. The central maximum is white. Continuous spectra are obtained at positions P and Q.

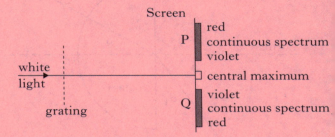

In the continuous spectra, violet is observed closest to the central maximum.

Which of the following statements is/are true?

   I Violet light has the shortest wavelength of all the visible radiations.

   II Violet light has the longest wavelength of all the visible radiations.

   III Violet light travels faster through air than the other visible radiations.

A I only

B II only

C III only

D I and III only

E II and III only

16. A ray of light passes from air into a substance that has a refractive index of 2·0. In air, the light has a wavelength λ and frequency f.

Which row in the following table gives the wavelength and frequency of the light in the substance?

	Wavelength	*Frequency*
A	λ	f
B	$\lambda/2$	$f/2$
C	$\lambda/2$	f
D	2λ	$2f$
E	2λ	f

[Turn over

17. The diagram below shows a ray of red light passing through a semicircular block of glass.

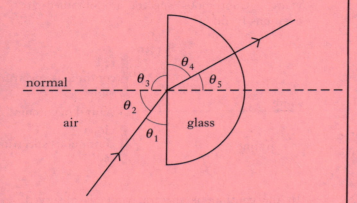

The refractive index of the glass for this light can be calculated from

A　$\dfrac{\sin \theta_3}{\sin \theta_4}$

B　$\dfrac{\sin \theta_1}{\sin \theta_4}$

C　$\dfrac{\sin \theta_2}{\sin \theta_5}$

D　$\dfrac{\sin \theta_2}{\sin \theta_4}$

E　$\dfrac{\sin \theta_1}{\sin \theta_5}$.

18. The statement below represents a nuclear reaction.

$$^{235}_{92}U + {}^{1}_{0}n \rightarrow {}^{92}_{36}Kr + {}^{141}_{56}Ba + {}^{1}_{0}n + {}^{1}_{0}n + {}^{1}_{0}n$$

This is an example of

A　nuclear fusion

B　alpha particle emission

C　beta particle emission

D　spontaneous nuclear fission

E　induced nuclear fission.

19. A radioactive source that emits gamma radiation is kept in a large container. A count rate of 160 counts per minute, after correction for background radiation, is recorded outside the container.

The container is to be shielded so that the corrected count rate at the same point outside the container is no more than 10 counts per minute.

Lead and water are available as shielding materials. For this source, the half-value thickness of lead is 11 mm and the half-value thickness of water is 110 mm.

Which of the following shielding arrangements will comply with the above requirement?

A　40 mm of lead only

B　33 mm of lead plus 110 mm of water

C　20 mm of lead plus 220 mm of water

D　11 mm of lead plus 275 mm of water

E　10 mm of lead plus 330 mm of water

20. The diagram below represents possible energy levels of an atom.

P _____ $-5 \cdot 2 \times 10^{-19}$ J

Q _____ $-9 \cdot 0 \times 10^{-19}$ J

R _____ $-16 \cdot 4 \times 10^{-19}$ J

S _____ $-24 \cdot 6 \times 10^{-19}$ J

Which of the following statements is/are true?

I There are four emission lines in the spectrum produced as a result of transitions between the energy levels shown.

II The radiation emitted with the shortest wavelength is produced by an electron falling from level P to level S.

III The zero energy level in an energy level diagram is known as the ionisation level.

A　I and II only

B　I and III only

C　II and III only

D　III only

E　I, II and III

SECTION B

Write your answers to questions 21 to 29 in the answer book.

Marks

21. At a funfair, a prize is awarded if a coin is tossed into a small dish. The dish is mounted on a shelf above the ground as shown.

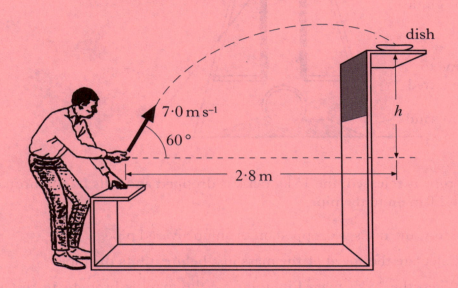

A contestant projects the coin with a speed of $7.0\,m\,s^{-1}$ at an angle of $60°$ to the horizontal. When the coin leaves his hand, the **horizontal distance** between the coin and the dish is $2.8\,m$. The coin lands in the dish.

The effect of air friction on the coin may be neglected.

(a) Calculate:

    (i)   the horizontal component of the initial velocity of the coin;

    (ii) the vertical component of the initial velocity of the coin.   **2**

(b) Show that the time taken for the coin to reach the dish is $0.8\,s$.   **1**

(c) What is the height, h, of the shelf above the point where the coin leaves the contestant's hand?   **2**

(d) How does the value of the kinetic energy of the coin when it enters the dish compare with the kinetic energy of the coin just as it leaves the contestant's hand?

    Justify your answer.   **2**

                                          (7)

[Turn over

Marks

22. The apparatus shown below is used to test concrete pipes.

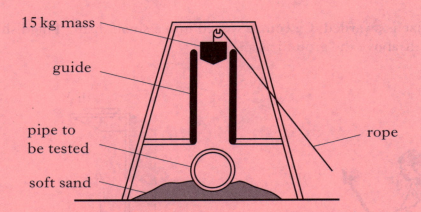

When the rope is released, the 15 kg mass is dropped and falls freely through a distance of 2·0 m on to the pipe.

(a) In one test, the mass is dropped on to an uncovered pipe.

   (i)   Calculate the speed of the mass just before it hits the pipe.

   (ii) When the 15 kg mass hits the pipe the mass is brought to rest in a time of 0·02 s. Calculate the size and direction of the average unbalanced force on the **pipe**.   5

(b) The same 15 kg mass is now dropped through the same distance on to an identical pipe which is covered with a thick layer of soft material.

   Describe and explain the effect this layer has on the size of the average unbalanced force on the pipe.   2

(c) Two 15 kg masses, X and Y, shaped as shown, are dropped through the same distance on to identical uncovered concrete pipes.

   When the masses hit the pipes, the masses are brought to rest in the same time.

   Which mass causes more damage to a pipe?

   Explain your answer in terms of pressure.   2

                                                                                          (9)

Marks

23. A sonar detector is attached to the bottom of a fresh water loch by a vertical cable as shown.

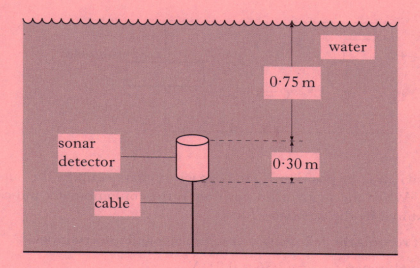

The detector has a mass of 100 kg. Each end of the detector has an area of 0·40 m². Atmospheric pressure is 101 000 Pa.

(a) The total pressure on the top of the detector is 108 350 Pa.

   Show that the total pressure on the bottom of the detector is 111 290 Pa.   **2**

(b) Calculate the upthrust on the detector.   **3**

(c) The sonar detector is now attached, as before, to the bottom of a **sea water** loch. The top of the detector is again 0·75 m below the surface of the water.

   How does the size of the upthrust on the detector now compare with your answer to (b)?

   You must justify your answer.   **2**

          (7)

[Turn over

Marks

24. (a) In an experiment to measure the capacitance of a capacitor, a student sets up the following circuit.

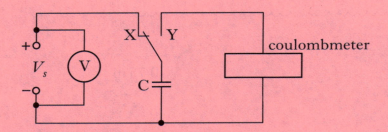

When the switch is in position X, the capacitor charges up to the supply voltage, V_s. When the switch is in position Y, the coulombmeter indicates the charge stored by the capacitor.

The student records the following measurements and uncertainties.

Reading on voltmeter $= (2{\cdot}56 \pm 0{\cdot}01)\,\text{V}$
Reading on coulombmeter $= (32 \pm 1)\,\mu\text{C}$

Calculate the value of the capacitance and the percentage uncertainty in this value. You must give the answer in the form

         value ± percentage uncertainty.   **3**

(b) The student designs the circuit shown below to switch off a lamp after a certain time.

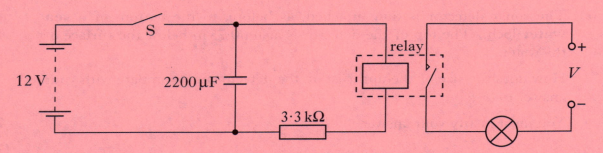

The 12 V battery has negligible internal resistance.

The relay contacts are normally open. When there is a current in the relay coil the contacts close and complete the lamp circuit.

Switch S is initially closed and the lamp is on.

  (i)   What is the maximum energy stored in the capacitor?

 (ii) (A)   Switch S is now opened. Explain why the lamp stays lit for a few seconds.

      (B)   The 2200 μF capacitor is replaced with a 1000 μF capacitor.

           Describe and explain the effect of this change on the operation of the circuit.   **6**

                                                                (9)

Marks

25. A photodiode is connected in a circuit as shown below.

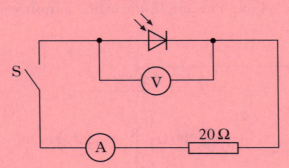

Switch S is open.

Light is shone on to the photodiode.

A reading is obtained on the voltmeter.

(a) (i)   State the mode in which the photodiode is operating.

 (ii)   Describe the effect of light on the material of which the photodiode is made.

 (iii)   The intensity of the light on the photodiode is increased.

 What happens to the reading on the voltmeter?   **3**

(b) Light of a constant intensity is shone on to the photodiode in the circuit shown above.

The following measurements are obtained with S open and then with S closed.

	S open	S closed
reading on voltmeter/V	0·508	0·040
reading on ammeter/mA	0·00	2·00

 (i)   What is the value of the e.m.f. produced by the photodiode for this light intensity?

 (ii)   Calculate the internal resistance of the photodiode for this light intensity.   **3**

(c) In the circuit above, the 20 Ω resistor is now replaced with a 10 Ω resistor.

The intensity of the light is unchanged.

The following measurements are obtained.

	S open	S closed
reading on voltmeter/V	0·508	0·021

Explain why the reading on the voltmeter, when S is closed, is smaller than the corresponding reading in part (b).   **2**

(8)

Marks

26. A circuit is set up as shown below. The amplitude of the output voltage of the a.c. supply is kept constant.

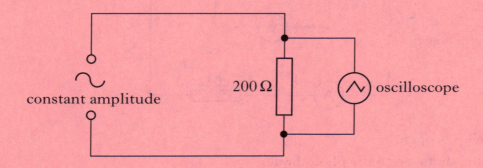

The settings of the controls on the oscilloscope are as follows:

y-gain setting   = 5 V/division
time-base setting = 2·5 ms/division

The following trace is displayed on the oscilloscope screen.

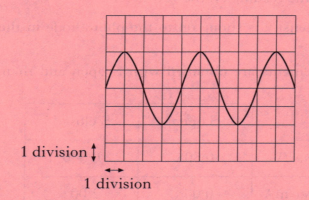

1 division ↕
← →
1 division

(*a*)   (i)   Calculate the frequency of the output from the a.c. supply.

(ii) Calculate the **r.m.s. current** in the 200 Ω resistor.   **5**

Marks

26.   (continued)

(*b*)   A diode is now connected in the circuit as shown below.

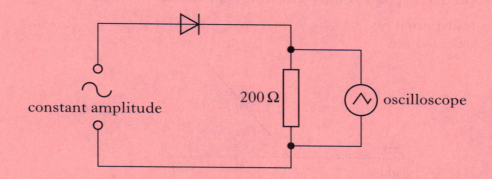

The settings on the controls of the oscilloscope remain unchanged.

Connecting the diode in the circuit causes **changes** to the original trace displayed on the oscilloscope screen. The new trace is shown below.

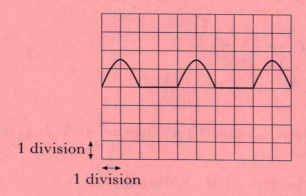

Describe and explain the changes to the original trace.

2

(7)

[Turn over

Marks

27. A student is investigating the effect that a semicircular glass block has on a ray of monochromatic light.

She observes that at point X the incident ray splits into two rays:

T — a transmitted ray
R — a reflected ray.

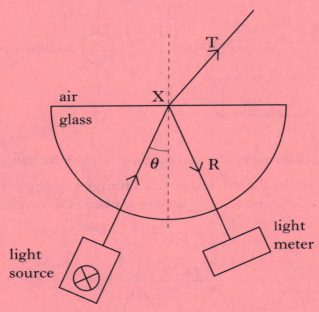

The student uses a light meter to measure the intensity of ray R as angle θ is changed.

(a) State what is meant by the *intensity* of a radiation.   1

(b) Explain why, as angle θ is changed, it is important to keep the light meter at a constant distance from point X for each measurement of intensity.   1

Marks

27. (continued)

(c) The graph below is obtained from the student's results.

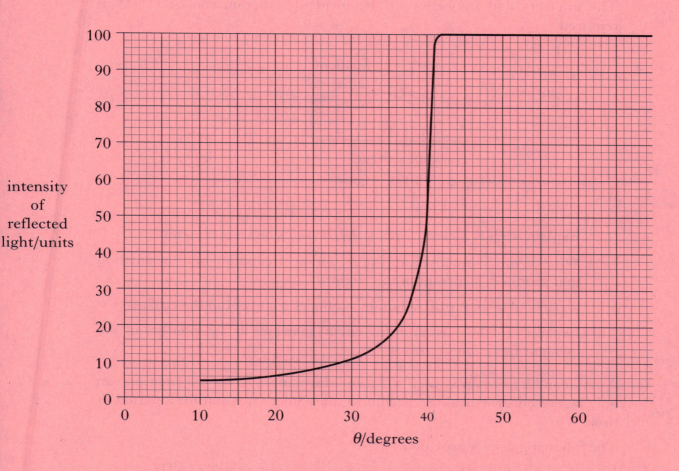

(i) What is the value of the critical angle in the glass for this light?

(ii) Calculate the refractive index of the glass for this light.

(iii) As the angle θ is increased, what happens to the intensity of ray T?   **4**

(6)

[Turn over

Marks

28. (*a*) The apparatus shown below is used to investigate photoelectric emission from a metal surface when electromagnetic radiation is shone on the surface.

The intensity and frequency of the incident radiation can be varied as required.

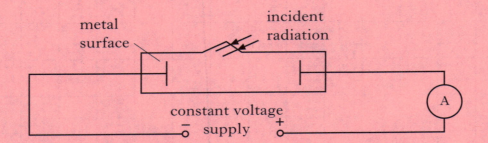

(i) Explain what is meant by *photoelectric emission* from a metal.

(ii) What is the name given to the minimum frequency of the radiation that produces a current in the circuit?

(iii) A particular source of radiation produces a current in the circuit.

Explain why the current in the circuit increases as the intensity of the incident radiation increases.

4

(*b*) A semiconductor chip is used to store information. The information can only be erased by exposing the chip to ultraviolet radiation for a period of time.

The following data is provided.

Frequency of ultraviolet radiation used   = $9 \cdot 0 \times 10^{14}\, Hz$

Minimum intensity of ultraviolet radiation
required at the chip   = $25\, W\, m^{-2}$

Area of the chip exposed to radiation   = $1 \cdot 8 \times 10^{-9}\, m^2$

Time taken to erase the information   = 15 minutes

Energy of radiation needed to erase the information = $40 \cdot 5\, \mu J$

(i) Calculate the energy of a photon of the ultraviolet radiation used.

(ii) Calculate the number of photons of the ultraviolet radiation required to erase the information.

(iii) Sunlight of intensity $25\, W\, m^{-2}$, at the chip, can also be used to erase the information.

State whether the time taken to erase the information is greater than, equal to or less than 15 minutes.

You must justify your answer.

5

(9)

Marks

29. Radium (Ra) decays to radon (Rn) by the emission of an alpha particle.

Some energy is also released by this decay.

The decay is represented by the statement shown below.

$$^{226}_{88}Ra \longrightarrow {}^{x}_{y}Rn + {}^{4}_{2}He$$

The masses of the nuclides involved are as follows.

Mass of $^{226}_{88}Ra$ = $3 \cdot 75428 \times 10^{-25}$ kg

Mass of $^{x}_{y}Rn$ = $3 \cdot 68771 \times 10^{-25}$ kg

Mass of $^{4}_{2}He$ = $6 \cdot 64832 \times 10^{-27}$ kg

(a) (i) What are the values of x and y for the nuclide $^{x}_{y}Rn$?

(ii) Why is energy released by this decay?

(iii) Calculate the energy released by one decay of this type.   5

(b) The alpha particle leaves the radium nucleus with a speed of $1 \cdot 5 \times 10^7 \, m \, s^{-1}$.

The alpha particle is now accelerated through a potential difference of 25 kV.

Calculate the **final** kinetic energy, in joules, of the alpha particle.   3

(8)

[END OF QUESTION PAPER]

[BLANK PAGE]

X069/301

NATIONAL
QUALIFICATIONS
2001

MONDAY, 4 JUNE
9.00 AM – 11.30 AM

PHYSICS
HIGHER

Read Carefully

1 All questions should be attempted.

Section A (questions 1 to 20)

2 Check that the answer sheet is for Physics Higher (Section A).

3 Answer the questions numbered 1 to 20 on the answer sheet provided.

4 Fill in the details required on the answer sheet.

5 Rough working, if required, should be done only on this question paper, or on the first two pages of the answer book provided—**not** on the answer sheet.

6 For each of the questions 1 to 20 there is only **one** correct answer and each is worth 1 mark.

7 Instructions as to how to record your answers to questions 1–20 are given on page three.

Section B (questions 21 to 29)

8 Answer questions numbered 21 to 29 in the answer book provided.

9 Fill in the details on the front of the answer book.

10 Enter the question number clearly in the margin of the answer book beside each of your answers to questions 21 to 29.

11 Care should be taken to give an appropriate number of significant figures in the final answers to calculations.

SCOTTISH
QUALIFICATIONS
AUTHORITY

DATA SHEET
COMMON PHYSICAL QUANTITIES

Quantity	Symbol	Value	Quantity	Symbol	Value
Speed of light in vacuum	c	$3 \cdot 00 \times 10^8$ m s^{-1}	Mass of electron	m_e	$9 \cdot 11 \times 10^{-31}$ kg
Magnitude of the charge on an electron	e	$1 \cdot 60 \times 10^{-19}$ C	Mass of neutron	m_n	$1 \cdot 675 \times 10^{-27}$ kg
Gravitational acceleration	g	$9 \cdot 8$ m s^{-2}	Mass of proton	m_p	$1 \cdot 673 \times 10^{-27}$ kg
Planck's constant	h	$6 \cdot 63 \times 10^{-34}$ J s			

REFRACTIVE INDICES

The refractive indices refer to sodium light of wavelength 589 nm and to substances at a temperature of 273 K.

Substance	Refractive index	Substance	Refractive index
Diamond	2·42	Water	1·33
Crown glass	1·50	Air	1·00

SPECTRAL LINES

Element	Wavelength/nm	Colour	Element	Wavelength/nm	Colour
Hydrogen	656	Red	Cadmium	644	Red
	486	Blue-green		509	Green
	434	Blue-violet		480	Blue
	410	Violet			
	397	Ultraviolet		Lasers	
	389	Ultraviolet	Element	Wavelength/nm	Colour
			Carbon dioxide	9550 } 10590 }	Infrared
Sodium	589	Yellow	Helium-neon	633	Red

PROPERTIES OF SELECTED MATERIALS

Substance	Density/ kg m^{-3}	Melting Point/ K	Boiling Point/ K
Aluminium	$2 \cdot 70 \times 10^3$	933	2623
Copper	$8 \cdot 96 \times 10^3$	1357	2853
Ice	$9 \cdot 20 \times 10^2$	273	. . . .
Sea Water	$1 \cdot 02 \times 10^3$	264	377
Water	$1 \cdot 00 \times 10^3$	273	373
Air	$1 \cdot 29$	. . . .	. . . .
Hydrogen	$9 \cdot 0 \times 10^{-2}$	14	20

The gas densities refer to a temperature of 273 K and a pressure of $1 \cdot 01 \times 10^5$ Pa.

SECTION A

For questions 1 to 20 in this section of the paper, an answer is recorded on the answer sheet by indicating the choice A, B, C, D or E by a stroke made in ink in the appropriate box of the answer sheet—see the example below.

EXAMPLE

The energy unit measured by the electricity meter in your home is the

    A   ampere

    B   kilowatt-hour

    C   watt

    D   coulomb

    E   volt.

The correct answer to the question is B—kilowatt-hour. Record your answer by drawing a heavy vertical line joining the two dots in the appropriate box on your answer sheet in the column of boxes headed B. The entry on your answer sheet would now look like this:

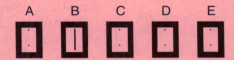

If after you have recorded your answer you decide that you have made an error and wish to make a change, you should cancel the original answer and put a vertical stroke in the box you now consider to be correct. Thus, if you want to change an answer D to an answer B, your answer sheet would look like this:

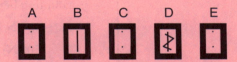

If you want to change back to an answer which has already been scored out, you should enter a tick (✓) to the RIGHT of the box of your choice, thus:

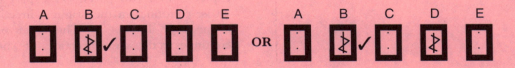

SECTION A

Answer questions 1–20 on the answer sheet.

1. Which one of the following pairs contains one vector quantity and one scalar quantity?

   A   Force, kinetic energy

   B   Power, speed

   C   Displacement, acceleration

   D   Work, potential energy

   E   Momentum, velocity

2. The diagram below shows the resultant of two vectors.

Which of the diagrams below shows the vectors which could produce the above resultant?

A

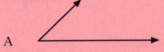

B

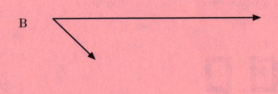

C

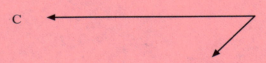

D

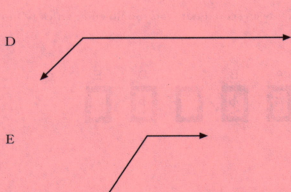

E

3. A helicopter is **descending** vertically at a constant speed of $3 \cdot 0 \, \text{m s}^{-1}$. A sandbag is released from the helicopter. The sandbag hits the ground $5 \cdot 0 \, \text{s}$ later.

What was the height of the helicopter above the ground at the time the sandbag was released?

   A $15 \cdot 0 \, \text{m}$

   B $49 \cdot 0 \, \text{m}$

   C $107 \cdot 5 \, \text{m}$

   D $122 \cdot 5 \, \text{m}$

   E $137 \cdot 5 \, \text{m}$

4. A car of mass $900 \, \text{kg}$ pulls a caravan of mass $400 \, \text{kg}$ along a straight, horizontal road with an acceleration of $2 \cdot 0 \, \text{m s}^{-2}$.

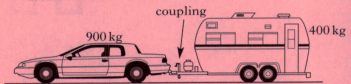

Assuming that the frictional forces on the caravan are negligible, the tension in the coupling between the car and the caravan is

   A $400 \, \text{N}$

   B $500 \, \text{N}$

   C $800 \, \text{N}$

   D $1800 \, \text{N}$

   E $2600 \, \text{N}$.

5. A rocket of mass $5 \cdot 0 \, \text{kg}$ is travelling horizontally with a speed of $200 \, \text{m s}^{-1}$ when it explodes into two parts. One part of mass $3 \cdot 0 \, \text{kg}$ continues in the original direction with a speed of $100 \, \text{m s}^{-1}$. The other part also continues in this same direction. Its speed is

   A $150 \, \text{m s}^{-1}$

   B $200 \, \text{m s}^{-1}$

   C $300 \, \text{m s}^{-1}$

   D $350 \, \text{m s}^{-1}$

   E $700 \, \text{m s}^{-1}$.

6. A block floats in water and two other liquids X and Y at the levels shown.

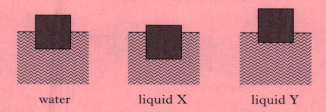

water   liquid X   liquid Y

Which of the following statements is/are correct?

   I The density of the material of the block is less than the density of water.

   II The density of liquid X is less than the density of water.

   III The density of liquid X is greater than the density of liquid Y.

   A   I only

   B   II only

   C   I and II only

   D   I and III only

   E   II and III only

7. Ice at −10 °C is heated until it becomes water at 80 °C.

   The temperature change on the kelvin scale is

   A   70 K

   B   90 K

   C   343 K

   D   363 K

   E   636 K.

8. In the diagrams below, each resistor has a resistance of 1·0 ohm.

   Select the combination which has the **least** value of effective resistance between the terminals X and Y.

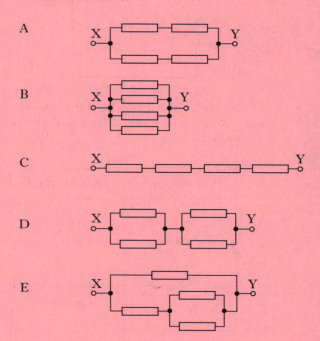

9. In the following circuit, the supply has negligible internal resistance.

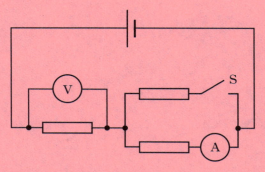

   Switch S is now closed.

   Which row in the table shows the effect on the ammeter and voltmeter readings?

	Ammeter reading	Voltmeter reading
A	increases	increases
B	increases	decreases
C	decreases	decreases
D	decreases	increases
E	decreases	remains the same

10. A supply with a sinusoidally alternating output of 6·0 V r.m.s. is connected to a 3·0 Ω resistor.

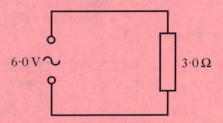

Which row in the following table shows the peak voltage across the resistor and the peak current in the circuit?

	Peak voltage/V	Peak current/A
A	$6\sqrt{2}$	$2\sqrt{2}$
B	$6\sqrt{2}$	2
C	6	2
D	$6\sqrt{2}$	$\dfrac{1}{2\sqrt{2}}$
E	6	$2\sqrt{2}$

11. A resistor and an ammeter are connected to a signal generator having an output of constant amplitude and variable frequency.

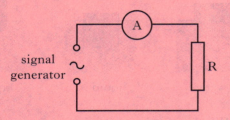

Which of the following graphs shows the correct relationship between the current I in the resistor and the output frequency f of the signal generator?

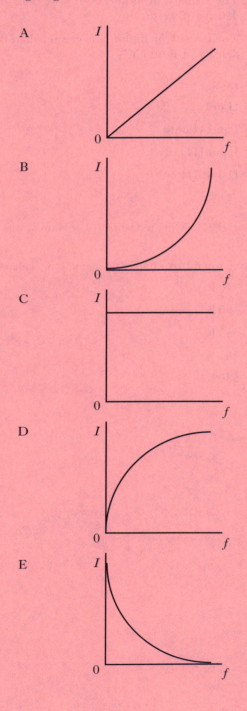

12. Which of the following statements is/are true for an ideal op-amp?

    I   It has infinite input resistance.

    II Both input pins are at the same potential.

    III The input current to the op-amp is zero.

  A   I only

  B   II only

  C   I and II only

  D   II and III only

  E   I, II and III

13. An op-amp circuit is shown in the diagram.

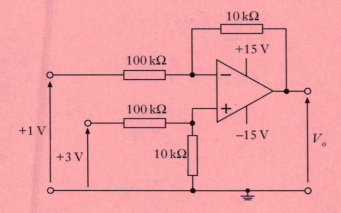

What is the output voltage V_o?

  A   −20 V

  B   −2 V

  C   −0·2 V

  D   0·2 V

  E   20 V

14. The energy of a water wave depends on its

  A   speed

  B   wavelength

  C   frequency

  D   period

  E   amplitude.

15. S_1 and S_2 are sources of coherent waves which produce an interference pattern along the line XY.

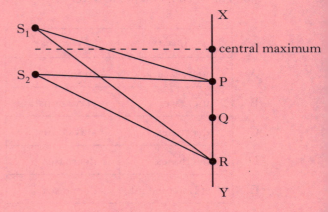

The first maximum occurs at P, where $S_1P = 20$ cm and $S_2P = 18$ cm.

For the third maximum, at R, the path difference $(S_1R - S_2R)$ is

  A   3 cm

  B   4 cm

  C   5 cm

  D   6 cm

  E   8 cm.

16. The spectrum of white light from a filament lamp may be viewed using a prism or a grating.

A student, asked to compare the spectra formed by the two methods, made the following statements.

    I The prism produces a spectrum by refraction. The grating produces a spectrum by interference.

    II The spectrum formed by the prism shows all the wavelengths present in the white light. The spectrum formed by the grating shows only a few specific wavelengths.

    III The prism produces a single spectrum. The grating produces more than one spectrum.

Which of the above statements is/are true?

  A   I only

  B   II only

  C   I and II only

  D   I and III only

  E   I, II and III

17. Red light passes from air into water.

What happens to the speed and frequency of the light when it enters the water?

	Speed	Frequency
A	increases	increases
B	increases	stays constant
C	decreases	stays constant
D	decreases	decreases
E	stays constant	decreases

18. The intensity of light from a point source is $20\,W\,m^{-2}$ at a distance of $5\cdot0\,m$ from the source.

What is the intensity of the light at a distance of $25\,m$ from the source?

A $0\cdot032\,W\,m^{-2}$

B $0\cdot80\,W\,m^{-2}$

C $1\cdot2\,W\,m^{-2}$

D $4\cdot0\,W\,m^{-2}$

E $100\,W\,m^{-2}$

19. Ultraviolet radiation causes the emission of photoelectrons from a zinc plate.

The intensity of the ultraviolet radiation is increased. Which row in the following table shows the effect of this change?

	Maximum kinetic energy of a photoelectron	Number of photoelectrons per second
A	increases	no change
B	no change	increases
C	no change	no change
D	increases	increases
E	decreases	increases

20. Under certain conditions, a nucleus of nitrogen absorbs an alpha particle to form the nucleus of another element and releases a single particle.

Which one of the following statements correctly describes this process?

A $^{14}_{7}N + \,^{3}_{2}He \rightarrow \,^{16}_{9}F + \,^{1}_{0}n$

B $^{14}_{7}N + \,^{4}_{2}He \rightarrow \,^{17}_{10}N + \,^{0}_{-1}e$

C $^{14}_{7}N + \,^{3}_{2}He \rightarrow \,^{16}_{8}O + \,^{1}_{1}p$

D $^{14}_{7}N + \,^{4}_{2}He \rightarrow \,^{18}_{9}F + 2\,^{0}_{-1}e$

E $^{14}_{7}N + \,^{4}_{2}He \rightarrow \,^{17}_{8}O + \,^{1}_{1}p$

SECTION B

Write your answers to questions 21 to 29 in the answer book.   *Marks*

21. (*a*) A box of mass 18 kg is at rest on a horizontal frictionless surface.
A force of 4·0 N is applied to the box at an angle of 26° to the horizontal.

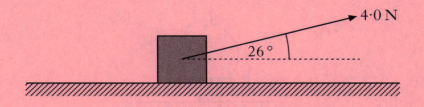

   (i)   Show that the horizontal component of this force is 3·6 N.

   (ii) Calculate the acceleration of the box along the horizontal surface.

   (iii) Calculate the horizontal distance travelled by the box in a time of
7·0 s.   **5**

(*b*) The box is replaced at rest at its starting position.

The force of 4·0 N is now applied to the box at an angle of less than 26° to
the horizontal.

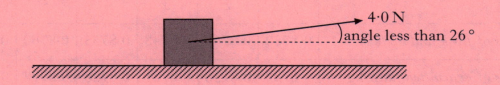

The force is applied for a time of 7·0 s as before.

How does the distance travelled by the box compare with your answer to
part (*a*)(iii)?

You must justify your answer.   **2**

                                                                           (7)

                                                                       [Turn over

22. (*a*) In an experiment to find the density of air, a student first measures the mass of a flask full of air as shown below.

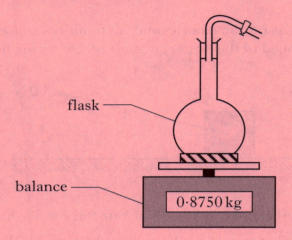

flask

balance

0·8750 kg

The air is now removed from the flask and the mass of the evacuated flask measured.

This procedure is repeated a number of times and the following table of measurements is obtained.

	Experiment number					
	1	2	3	4	5	6
Mass of flask and air/kg	0·8750	0·8762	0·8748	0·8755	0·8760	0·8757
Mass of evacuated flask/kg	0·8722	0·8736	0·8721	0·8728	0·8738	0·8732
Mass of air removed/kg						

The volume of the flask is measured as $2 \cdot 0 \times 10^{-3}$ m^3.

(i) Copy and complete the **bottom row** of the table.

(ii) Calculate the mean mass of air removed from the flask **and** the random uncertainty in this mean. Express the mean mass and the random uncertainty in kilograms.

(iii) Use these measurements to calculate the density of air.

(iv) Another student carries out the same experiment using a flask of larger volume.

Explain why this is a better design for the experiment.   **6**

Marks

22.   (continued)

(*b*) The cylinder of a bicycle pump has a length of 360 mm as shown in the diagram.

The outlet of the pump is sealed.

The piston is pushed inwards until it is 160 mm from the outlet.

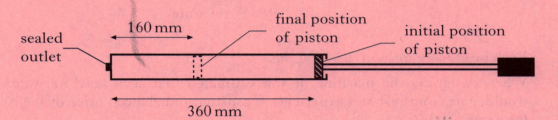

The initial pressure of the air in the pump is $1 \cdot 0 \times 10^5$ Pa.

 (i)   Assuming that the temperature of the air trapped in the cylinder remains constant, calculate the final pressure of the trapped air.

 (ii) State one other assumption you have made for this calculation.

 (iii) Use the kinetic model to explain what happens to the pressure of the trapped air as its volume decreases.

5

(11)

[Turn over

Marks

23. Beads of liquid moving at high speed are used to move threads in modern weaving machines.

(a) In one design of machine, beads of water are accelerated by jets of air as shown in the diagram.

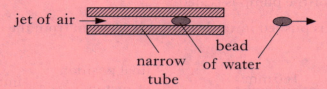

jet of air →

narrow tube

bead of water

Each bead has a mass of 2.5×10^{-5} kg.

When designing the machine, it was estimated that each bead of water would start from rest and experience a constant unbalanced force of 0·5 N for a time of 3·0 ms.

(i) Calculate:

(A) the impulse on a bead of water;

(B) the speed of the bead as it emerges from the tube.

(ii) In practice the force on a bead varies.

The following graph shows how the actual unbalanced force exerted on each bead of water varies with time.

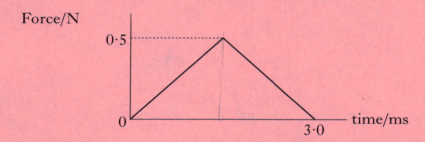

Use information from this graph to show that the bead leaves the tube with a speed equal to half of the value calculated in part (i)(B).   **6**

(b) Another design of machine uses beads of oil and two metal plates X and Y.

The potential difference between these plates is 5.0×10^{3} V.

Each bead of oil has a mass of 4.0×10^{-5} kg and is given a negative charge of 6.5×10^{-6} C.

The bead accelerates from rest at plate X and passes through a hole in plate Y.

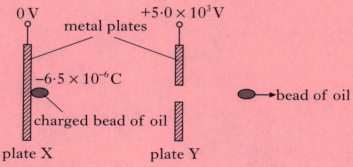

Neglecting air friction, calculate the speed of the bead at plate Y.   **3**

(9)

Marks

24. (*a*) The following circuit is used to measure the e.m.f. and the internal resistance of a battery.

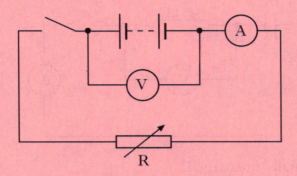

Readings of current and potential difference from this circuit are used to produce the following graph.

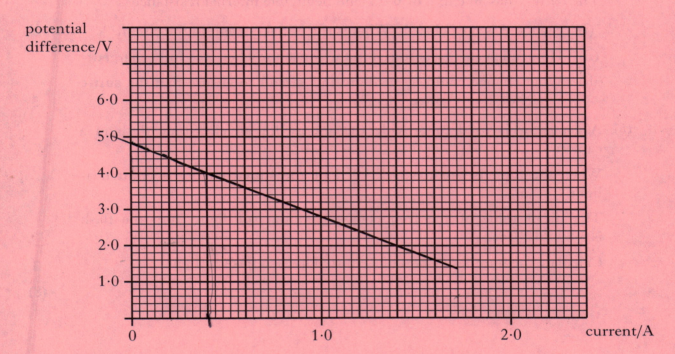

Use information from the graph to find:

(i)   the e.m.f. of the battery, in volts;

(ii) the internal resistance of the battery.   **3**

(*b*) A car battery has an e.m.f. of 12 V and an internal resistance of $0.050\,\Omega$.

(i)   Calculate the short circuit current for this battery.

(ii) The battery is now connected in series with a lamp. The resistance of the lamp is $2.5\,\Omega$. Calculate the power dissipated in the lamp.   **5**

(8)

[Turn over

Marks

25. (*a*) The following diagram shows a circuit that is used to investigate the charging of a capacitor.

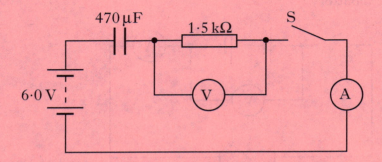

The capacitor is initially uncharged.

The capacitor has a capacitance of $470\,\mu\text{F}$ and the resistor has a resistance of $1\cdot5\,\text{k}\Omega$.

The battery has an e.m.f. of $6\cdot0\,\text{V}$ and negligible internal resistance.

  (i)   Switch S is now closed. What is the initial current in the circuit?

  (ii) How much energy is stored in the capacitor when it is fully charged?

  (iii) What change could be made to this circuit to ensure that the **same** capacitor stores **more** energy?   5

(*b*) A capacitor is used to provide the energy for an electronic flash in a camera.

When the flash is fired, $6\cdot35 \times 10^{-3}\,\text{J}$ of the stored energy is emitted as light.

The mean value of the frequency of photons of light from the flash is $5\cdot80 \times 10^{14}\,\text{Hz}$.

Calculate the number of photons emitted in each flash of light.   3

                            (8)

Marks

26. (a) An op-amp is connected in a circuit as shown below.

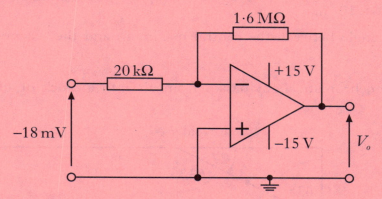

(i)   In which mode is the op-amp operating?

(ii) A voltage of −18 mV is connected to the input. Calculate the output voltage V_o.

(iii) The supply voltage is now reduced from ±15 V to ±12 V.

State any effect this change has on the output voltage. You must justify your answer.   4

(b) A student connects an op-amp as shown in the following diagram. An alternating voltage of peak value 5·0 V is connected to the input as shown.

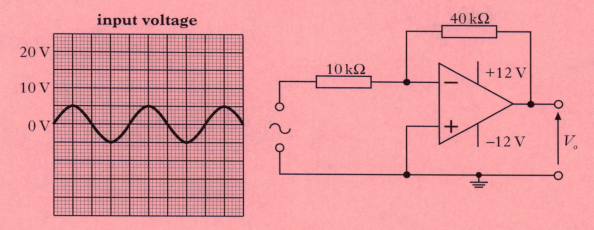

The sketch below shows the student's attempt to draw the corresponding output voltage.

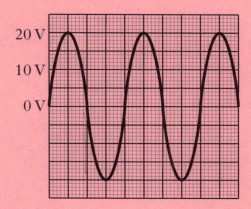

State the **two** mistakes in the student's sketch.   2

(6)

Marks

27. (*a*) Light of wavelength 486×10^{-9} m is viewed using a grating with a slit spacing of $2 \cdot 16 \times 10^{-6}$ m.

Calculate the angle between the central maximum and the second order maximum.   **2**

(*b*) A ray of monochromatic light passes from air into a block of glass as shown.

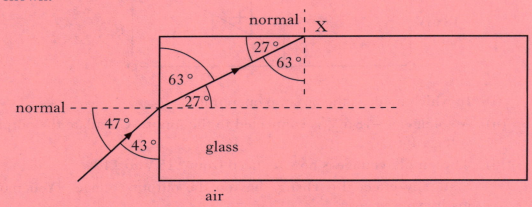

(i) Using information from the diagram, show that the refractive index of the glass for this light is 1·61.

(ii) Show by calculation whether the ray is totally internally reflected at point X.   **4**

                                                                                          (6)

Marks

28. (*a*) In a laser, the light is produced by stimulated emission of radiation.

Explain the term "stimulated emission" by making reference to the energy levels in atoms.

2

(*b*) A laser beam is shone on to a screen which is marked with a grid.

The beam produces a uniformly lit spot of radius 5.00×10^{-4} m as shown.

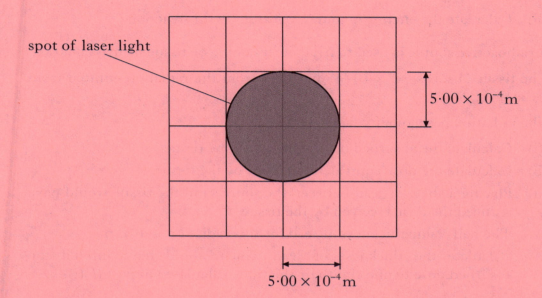

spot of laser light

5.00×10^{-4} m

5.00×10^{-4} m

(i) The intensity of the spot of light on the screen is $1020\,\text{W}\,\text{m}^{-2}$.

Calculate the power of the laser beam.

(ii) The distance between the screen and the laser is now doubled.

State how the radius of the spot now compares with the one shown in the diagram.

You must justify your answer.

5

(7)

[Turn over

Marks

29. (*a*) The following statement represents a nuclear reaction.

$$^{239}_{94}Pu + ^{1}_{0}n \longrightarrow ^{137}_{52}Te + ^{100}_{42}Mo + 3^{1}_{0}n + energy$$

The total mass of the particles before the reaction is $3 \cdot 9842 \times 10^{-25}$ kg and the total mass of the particles after the reaction is $3 \cdot 9825 \times 10^{-25}$ kg.

  (i) State and explain whether this reaction is spontaneous or induced.

 (ii) Calculate the energy, in joules, released by this reaction.   **3**

(*b*) A radioactive source is used to irradiate a sample of tissue of mass $0 \cdot 50$ kg.

The tissue absorbs $9 \cdot 6 \times 10^{-5}$ J of energy from the radiation emitted from the source.

The radiation has a quality factor of 1.

  (i) Calculate the absorbed dose received by the tissue.

 (ii) Calculate the dose equivalent received by the tissue.

(iii) Placing a sheet of lead between the source and the tissue would have reduced the dose received by the tissue.

      The half-value thickness of lead for this radiation is 40 mm.

      Calculate the thickness of lead which would have limited the absorbed dose to one eighth of the value calculated in part (*b*)(i).   **5**

                                                            (8)

[END OF QUESTION PAPER]

[BLANK PAGE]

[BLANK PAGE]

[BLANK PAGE]

[BLANK PAGE]